OUR LAST MISSION

Lawrence I. Pifer, 1943. Courtesy of Lawrence Pifer.

Our Last Mission

A World War II Prisoner in Germany

Dawn Trimble Bunyak

Foreword by Arnold Krammer

University of Oklahoma Press : Norman

This book is published with the generous assistance of The McCasland Foundation, Duncan, Oklahoma.

Library of Congress Cataloging-in-Publication Data

Bunyak, Dawn.
    Our last mission : a World War II prisoner in Germany / Dawn Trimble Bunyak ; foreword by Arnold Krammer.
       p.   cm.
    Includes bibliographical references and index.
    ISBN 0-8061-3547-6 (hc : alk. paper)
    1. Pifer, Lawrence I.   2. World War, 1939–1945—Prisoners and prisons, German.   3. United States. Army Air Forces—Airmen—Biography.   4. Prisoners of war—Germany—Biography.   5. Prisoners of war—United States—Biography. I. Pifer, Lawrence I.   II. Title.

D805.G3B86   2003
940.54'7243'092—dc21
[B]

2003042664

The paper in this book meets the guidelines for permanence and durability of the Committee on Production Guidelines for Book Longevity of the Council on Library Resources, Inc. ∞

1 2 3 4 5 6 7 8 9 10

To my hero, Lawrence Pifer,
and to all the ex-American prisoners of war
who know the true meaning of freedom

CONTENTS

Illustrations

FIGURES

• • •

FOREWORD

There is astonishingly little written about the history of prisoners of war, especially when one considers the numbers involved. During World War II about eighty million people served in various battling armies, and while the exact figures will probably never be known, an estimated thirty-five million spent time as prisoners of war in enemy hands. Many died in captivity and all suffered the indignities, boredom, and cruelty often meted out by poor-quality guards. Yet, public interest in war prisoners was slow to evolve. People simply weren't concerned about them. The number of early books and studies about these abandoned souls are surprisingly few, and came to light haltingly. Public attention depended largely on the liberalization of each country's cultural view toward war prisoners, Japan being the most recalcitrant.

The reasons for this initial disinterest are clear and entirely human. First, the Big Picture consumed the postwar public—the lure of new products, concepts, and opportunities. Books about major battles, generals, weapons, and global strategies flooded the market, as did biographies of Churchill, Hitler, Rommel, Eisenhower, MacArthur, and Nimitz. Bestsellers about the battles of Normandy, the Bulge, and Britain competed on the shelves with rosy predictions of the new postwar era. The few portraits of ordinary soldiers were to be found in brilliant fiction by returning combat veterans like Norman Mailer (*The Naked and the Dead*), James Jones (*From Here to Eternity*), Robert Lee Scott (*God Is My Co-Pilot*), Kurt Vonnegut (*Slaughterhouse Five*), and James Michener (*Tales of the South Pacific*).[1]

Yet, the number of books about the experiences of prisoners of war could be counted on one hand: Edward Beattie's raw and anguished *Diary of a Kriegie* (1946), Alan Newcomb's *Vacation with Pay: Being an Account of My Stay at the German Rest Camp for Tired Allied Airmen at Beautiful Barth-on-the-Baltic* (1947)—whose caustically humorous title parodies his ill-treatment as well as his nation's lack of support. The following year, 1948, saw publication of *Paratrooper Padre*, a conflicted account by Francis Sampson, whose experiences in an elite combat unit challenged his calling as a man of the cloth. Finally, in 1951, an excellent, albeit limited, account by John Vietor appeared as *Time Out: American Airmen at Stalag Luft I*. The single academic study was an estimable, although unheralded and unpublished, master's thesis by Ben Goldman titled "German Treatment of American Prisoners of War in World War II" (Wayne State University, 1949).[2]

The second reason for the early lack of interest in the story of prisoners of war stemmed from the traditional military view of soldiers who fall into enemy hands. Since biblical times, war captives had been considered property and counted as war booty to be enslaved or killed. The opposing army that lost the prisoner viewed its loss as expendable and considered its former soldiers as potential turncoats who might be pressured into revealing military information to the enemy. Captured war prisoners were considered cowards by both sides, undeserving of concern or further interest. Neither side was moved to allocate precious resources for their care or upkeep. War hysteria and cultural attitudes further influenced their poor treatment, and as recently as World War II the fate of Allied prisoners in Japanese hands or Germans in Russian captivity was little more than a slow death sentence. Until very recently, medals or public acknowledgment for former war prisoners were unthinkable. It was the Vietnam War, media-driven and polarizing, that caused the American public to reevaluate the plight of its sons and brothers, heroic and clearly loyal, as they fell into the hands of an inscrutable and apparently unyielding distant enemy.

That is not to say that no one was concerned with the experiences of war prisoners during the first years following World War II. Military archivists, sensitive to the erosion of memory and determined to document the ill-treatment of Americans in enemy hands, collected documents and conducted interviews with former prisoners. Most remain untouched, except on occasion by scholars, and are gathering dust.[3] A few articles appeared in the popular press—the *Saturday Evening Post* and *Atlantic Monthly*—and in *Aerospace Historian* and the *Department of State Bulletin*. There was even a chirpy 1946 article on "My Christmas in a German Prisoner of War Camp" in *Better Homes and Gardens*.

Otherwise, the public was not confronted with the POW issue until 1953, when it was thrust onto the screen in an Academy Award-winning movie, *Stalag 17*. Although the plot is vintage McCarthy-era fare about a German spy working from within a group of American POWs, secretly disclosing their escape plans to the enemy, the public was forced to face the spartan conditions of POW life and the often life-and-death problems facing brave and stereotypical American soldiers in a nameless prison camp. That year the reading public snapped up two new books, *P.O.W.*, by a former B-24 gunner, Edward Dobran, who spent a year in Stalag Luft IV, and a general, wide-ranging book by Eric Williams, *The Book of Famous Escapes*.[4] The public was clearly ready to take the next step. That step came in the form of the blockbuster movie about the brutality of life in a remote Japanese POW camp, *Bridge on the River Kwai* (1957). Alec Guinness and Sessue Hayakawa play an eyeball-to-eyeball cat-and-mouse game of devotion to duty and hubris in the form of building a crucial bridge that is ultimately destroyed, together with the Japanese chances of military success and the honor of the Japanese commandant. The movie garnered seven Academy Awards, opened America's eyes to the horrors of prison camp life, and gave the public a whistling marching tune that remained popular for decades.

Prisoner-of-war movies were almost becoming fashionable. One, like the 1962 Cold War thriller, *The Manchurian Candidate*, utilized brain-washed American POWs during the Korean War to point out the dangers of international Communism. But the trend was clearly to focus on life in enemy prison camps, shorn of politics. In 1963 another blockbuster hit the screens: *The Great Escape*, with Steve McQueen. The film is based on the true story of seventy-six Allied POWs who escaped from Stalag Luft III in March 1944 after a year of digging shafts, counterfeiting documents, tailoring enemy uniforms, and maintaining a camp security system as complicated as the proverbial Swiss watch. Indeed, *The Great Escape* is still among the most popular movies available.

No sooner had the dust settled from *The Great Escape* than yet another excellent POW film appeared in 1965: *King Rat*. In this movie, based on James Clavell's real experiences in a Japanese camp, an undisciplined American corporal (George Segal) rises from a camp scrounger and wheeler-dealer to a successful entrepreneur who cultivates a secret rat farm under the barracks, unbeknownst to his starving officers who buy the meat disguised as a local delicacy. The American public was now clearly ready to face the experiences of the ninety-five thousand U.S. prisoners who spent part or all of the war years in enemy captivity. What the public got, however, was a ludicrous television series called *Hogan's Heroes* (1965–74).

Hogan's Heroes was a zany situation comedy in which American Air Force Colonel Hogan leads a small band of misfit POWs in a nameless German camp to befuddle and corrupt the ever-confused Colonel Klink and his jovial Sergeant Schultz. By using threats, flattery, and sleight-of-hand, Hogan contacts the "local Resistance fighters" at will, smuggles secrets to London, and generally sabotages the German military effort with apparent ease. Sidestepping a torrent of criticism from every direction, particularly from former POWs who were outraged at the trivialization of their experiences, *Hogan's Heroes* flourished for nine years and, in fact, continues in syndication to this moment.

Suddenly, in the midst of the public's growing interest in the fate of its prisoners of war, a sobering event caused confusion. The horrors revealed by Israel's trial of Nazi war criminal Adolf Eichmann in 1961 gave full understanding to the new use of *Holocaust* in the world's lexicon. The mass murder of Europe's Jews by the Nazis was certainly well known before the Eichmann trial, but Jewish communities had somehow seen these murders as disjointed individual tragedies rather than as a huge state-managed genocidal program that involved most segments of German industry, military, and government. Historians, for their part, had mostly viewed the Holocaust as part of the military war, rather than as the separate, obsessive extermination program Eichmann revealed it to have been. Holocaust studies went on to become a separate and highly respected discipline, and surviving Jews worldwide learned the gravity of industrial anti-Semitism and resolved to protect themselves in the future, but the American public was understandably confused.

What was the difference between prisoner-of-war camps and concentration camps? The documentary concentration camp scenes of strutting guards, barbed wire fences, and sentry towers blurred with pictures of American POW camps, showing similar guards, fences, and towers. Moreover, *Hogan's Heroes* made it all look like fun. The public no longer knew one type of camp from another, and many do not to this day. That bewilderment was compounded by the unfamiliar terms used by each type of camp system, particularly POW camps. While concentration camps were simply abbreviated *KZ* or *KL* for the German word *Konzentrationslager* (as in KZ Auschwitz, or KL Dachau), the POW camps were divided into concentrations of airmen or ground troops, permanent or transit, officers or enlisted men. Thus, *Lager* was the German equivalent of any camp, and Stalag was the abbreviation for *Stammlager* or permanent army camp for enlisted men. Oflag was the abbreviation for *Offizierslager* or permanent officers' camp, and Dulag was short for *Durchgangslager* or transit camp. Any POW camp operated by the *Luftwaffe*, or air force, for downed Allied fliers was simply called a Stalag Luft, whether for POW officers or enlisted men. Finally, the official German term for prisoners of war was *Kriegsgefangene*, a real tongue twister for most American boys. Hence, Allied POWs simply referred to themselves forever after as "Kriegies."

The 1960s witnessed a growing interest in the experience of American POWs following the release of such popular films as noted above and the ongoing lunacy of *Hogan's Heroes*. More books appeared, three of the best being *Name, Rank, and Serial Number* (1969) by Florimond Duke, *Prisoners of War* (1975) by A. J. Barker, and *A Holiday in Hitlerland* (1970) by James F. Stone, a former bombardier and Luft I Kriegie whose now-familiar sarcastic title belies his tribulations in enemy hands. In 1967 the theme of prisoners was viewed through the psychedelic lens of the Age of Aquarius to produce a quirky British-made TV show starring Patrick MacGoohan called *The Prisoner* (1967, in U.S., 1968). Although the convoluted, dark story about the interrogation of agent Number Six lasted only seventeen episodes, the show has achieved cult status today.[5]

By the mid-1960s the heavily televised war in Vietnam brought home the plight of American POWs in Southeast Asia, and the public began to see them as individuals rather than as a category of expendable or cowardly soldiers. It became fashionable to wear the name of a single POW on a metal bracelet. Prisoners who were fortunate enough to be released from captivity wrote their memoirs and many used their popularity to catapult themselves into local and national politics. Only one year after the end of the Vietnam War, an excellent book appeared from John G. Hubbell titled *P.O.W.: A Definitive History of the American Prisoner-of-War Experience in Vietnam, 1964–1973.*[6] Three years later American television broadcast a major film, *When Hell Was in Session* (1979), the true story of navy commander Jeremiah Denton's horrific seven and one-half years in a North Vietnamese POW camp and his heroic and ultimately uplifting efforts to unite his fellow prisoners while maintaining their sanity under the most adverse conditions.

Meanwhile, archives were declassifying documents dealing with the POWs, and periodic anniversaries of V-E and V-J Day stirred the embers of recollections by participants. The best single book about Americans in the European Theater appeared from scholar David A. Foy, titled *For You the War Is Over: American Prisoners of War in Nazi Germany* (1984). The following year, 1985, saw the publication of the notable book by E. B. Kerr about the Pacific Theater, *Surrender and Survival: The Experience of American POWs in the Pacific—1941–1945.* Pedestrian books appeared over the next several years until the publication in 1991 of the splendid recollection by David Westheimer, *Sitting It Out: A World War II POW Memoir.* Westheimer, who is Jewish, had the additional worry that the Germans or his bigoted American comrades would learn about his religion. Arthur Durand wrote an excellent, still unpublished, Ph.D. dissertation, "Stalag Luft III: An American Experience in a World War II German Prisoner of War Camp" (Louisiana State University, 1976). The Veteran's Administration released its "Study of Former Prisoners of War" (Studies and Analysis Service, Office of Planning and Program Evaluation, 1980). Finally, an incisive book appeared in 1993 which indicated, perhaps, that the initial literary phase of POW studies—the contribution of primary recollections—was evolving into a more mature, contemplative stage. The book was Robert C. Doyle's *Voices from Captivity: Interpreting the American POW Narrative*.[7]

Once again, moviemakers began to turn to POW stories as an untapped venue. Sylvester Stallone starred in a forgettable movie called *Victory* (1981), in which a group of Nazi officers devise a propaganda event to challenge their all-star Nazi soccer team against their POWs in a winner-take-all game. With the help of the Brazilian World Cup Champion, Pelé, the POWs win and ultimately escape. In 1983, British media icon David Bowie gave a credible performance in *Merry Christmas, Mr. Lawrence*, a film depicting the complicated relationship between a British officer and his Japanese camp commander in a POW camp in Java. Most recently (2002), tough guy Bruce Willis discovered the potential of a POW setting in *Hart's War*, in which an American colonel, William McNamara, utilizes a camp murder to demand a formal court-martial officiated by the German SS camp commandant while McNamara secretly plots the destruction of a nearby German munitions factory. In 1993, a made-for-television movie, *Stalag Luft*, entered the nation's living rooms and the vast American public once again realized the importance of this aspect of the history of World War II. Finally, on November 8, 1985, the seemingly unthinkable happened. Congress passed Public Law 99-145 authorizing an official medal be awarded to every former POW dating back to April 1917. The subject of American POWs had entered the mainstream.

Believe it or not, the ubiquitous *Hogan's Heroes* currently flourishes on German television. The German-language version takes parody a step further. Now called *Ein Kafig Voller Helden* (*A Cage Full of Heroes*), Col. Klink and Sgt. Schultz have rural Gomer Pyle-type accents, stiff-armed salutes are accompanied by such witticisms as "this is how high the cornflowers grow," references are made to Col. Klink's maid who cleans in the nude, and "bombs" dropped on London are translated as "condoms." How rich the irony: German fans of a comedy that ridicules Germans, lionizes Germany's former enemies, and trivializes the gravity of the circumstances. Perhaps the topic has been fully digested after all.

It is axiomatic that every soldier, and POW, experiences a different war. Each knows only the three meters around him. That knowledge alone distinguishes every book of recollections. So, too, every POW camp was different, depending on the quality of the guards, the weather and climate, the attitude of the enemy commandant, and the closeness to the end of the war. All these aspects are critical to any story about American POWs in Germany. There were a total of fifty-seven large Stalag, Stalag Lufts, and Oflag POW camps in Germany during the war, many holding 3,000 to 5,500 men or more.

The book you are about to read is unique. It might not seem so at first glance. After all, Sergeant Larry Pifer was not unlike every young flier in the war; he wasn't a professional soldier, just one of millions who came of age in a turbulent time. He came from the hamlet of Clearfield, in mid-Pennsylvania, perhaps best known for being the town nearest Punxsutawney, where America's famous groundhog, "Punxsutawney Phil," is annually called upon to predict the arrival of spring. Two years after he graduated from high school at age seventeen, young Larry Pifer enlisted in the Army Air Corps. He received routine training, was assigned the especially dangerous job as a ball gunner in a B-17, and put into an airplane like so many thousands of other young men. The similarity ended when his plane was blown out of the sky at eighteen thousand feet on a bombing mission over Berlin in March 1944, when he saw a number of his buddies killed before his eyes, and a young, wounded Larry Pifer parachuted into hostile territory.

Surviving the immediate dangers of angry civilians and undisciplined armed soldiers, Pifer was interrogated for days, locked in a tiny cold cell, and then loaded with hundreds of other Allied captives into crowded cattle cars to be transported to the huge Dulag Luft transit camp in Berlin. Larry joined the two thousand new POWs who arrived every month at the Dulag. He began his fourteen months in a prison camp system five thousand miles from home. Bombed, starved, and terrorized, the young airman from Clearfield, Pennsylvania, eventually landed in his temporary new home—Stalag Luft VI—located near the old Prussian-Lithuanian border, not far from the turbulent northern Baltic Sea.

It was the final year of the war. Food was scarce, the German guards were unruly and especially dangerous, and the vengeful Red Army was pouring out of Russia into eastern Europe. The winter cold was brutal. The German war effort was collapsing, and the thousands of sick and starving Allied POWs at Stalag VI were in the path of the chaos. An increasing number of escapes brought in the tyrannical SS troops, who then, under the worst conditions, lashed long lines of straggling POWs westward in forced marches into the final German stronghold. Sergeant Larry Pifer, limping and skeletal, was there throughout, and remembers it all—the squabbles between hungry prisoners, the heartening war news, the nearly unheard-of gesture of friendship from a worried guard, American POWs killed for being unable to maintain the evacuation pace, names and events from his diary, stretching the contents of a rare Red Cross package, and the countless colored threads in the tapestry of enforced confinement. But, imprisonment is only part of Larry's story. On July 12, 1944, the prisoners at Stalag VI were shackled and marched inland to Stalag Luft IV, one hundred miles northeast of Berlin, and again, one step ahead of the Russians, they were evacuated to Stalag 11-B, where they endured to await liberation.

Liberation arrived in a British uniform on May 2, 1945. Euphoria and bewilderment were intertwined as Larry and thousands of newly liberated POWs were gingerly fed and brought back to health. Enemy troops were divided as some surrendered and others fought on. Larry describes the chaos as the POWs were transported toward the so-called "cigarette camps" in France to await the availability of American Liberty Ships that would carry them home.

Home at last. Unlike most histories of the POW experience, which end abruptly with liberation, Larry's recollections take him back to his roots, to the beginning of the story. Clearfield, Pennsylvania. Less than two months after his liberation from a German prisoner-of-war camp, he found himself in a different world, in the midst of welcomes and nightmares and a sudden reintegration into life on the Home Front, with concerns about ration books, war bonds, and the latest news about the Pacific campaign and the pending invasion of Japan. Being physically touched was excruciating; he couldn't talk about his experiences; and after so many months of being crammed in camps, Larry craved space and silence. Old friends were like strangers. He traveled aimlessly to visit old comrades. As the meaningless months dragged on, Larry knew he faced a crossroads. Like returning soldiers since time immemorial, he found that he couldn't function in his old environment any longer. He had seen too much.

And like thousands of veterans before him, he longed for the structure, brotherhood, and shared danger of men who had been through similar experiences. In May 1947, Sergeant Lawrence Pifer reenlisted in the U.S. Army Air Corps.

This isn't the story of the Big Picture so prevalent after the war, or an angry indictment by a newly repatriated former POW. Larry Pifer's recollections are unique. His story about growing up at the end of the Great Depression in a small town in middle America, responding to his country's call, being shot down and surviving the rigors of enemy captivity, and returning to a home life that he could no longer understand—is different. It is honest and detailed, admirably interpreted by his niece, Dawn Bunyak, and has the important benefit of nearly fifty years of reflection. The passage of time has allowed Larry Pifer to weigh events from the distance of maturity and compare them with other life experiences. Events are no longer colored by wartime hatred, by the frustrations and depression that come with prolonged captivity, or by the indescribable exhilaration and bewilderment of freedom—and the uncomfortable return home.

This unique memoir belongs in every collection of World War II studies.

ARNOLD KRAMMER

PREFACE

In World War II, ninety-four thousand American men were interned in prisoner-of-war camps in Europe and nearly thirty thousand men and women in the Pacific Theater. These brave Americans, most in their teens and twenties, suffered weeks, months, even years of torture, disease, and starvation. The imprisoned waited for death, liberation, or an end to the conflict. Freedom took on a special meaning for these Americans. As Allied troops advanced into territories earlier held by the Axis powers, captors released men, women, and children detained in prison and concentration camps around the world. The American ex-prisoners traveled to the United States by ships and planes and eventually by trains and cars to their hometowns.

Naïve youths, who enlisted in the armed services filled with patriotism and dreams of adventure often returned troubled, depressed, and paranoid. Debriefed and honorably discharged, the former prisoners of war struggled alone to move on with their lives and leave the past behind. Nightmares and memories haunted them. Physically and emotionally scarred, they struggled for years, decades, even whole lifetimes, to reconcile themselves to the events that had stolen their innocence and youth and left them old before their time. For some, the emotional struggle was too much and they took their own lives. Others were able to close the door on the nightmares and memories; they found jobs, married, and raised families. Quite unexpectedly, however, an event or a reunion, a meeting with a forgotten army buddy, or even a sound, could release a torrent of memories. The experiences of war could haunt former POWs forever.

As they aged, many soldiers, airmen, and nurses of the World War II generation sought out old comrades to discuss the life-altering events of their youth. They found that many of them had died. Others preferred to forget that time in their lives. Veterans' hospitals that treated men and women for post-traumatic stress after the Vietnam conflict created encounter groups for World War II veterans as well. Chaplains and counselors helped troubled veterans find inner peace and acceptance by facing issues through discussion with other veterans and trained professionals. Spouses were invited to join separate encounter groups to work through issues that had troubled them over the many years of their marriages.

After counseling, many ex-POWs found that they could share their memories with family, friends, and others who were willing to listen. Many of them visited schools to speak about their experiences during World War II. Reunions of ex-prisoners were organized across the country, and, to find closure, some veterans traveled to Europe and the Pacific to visit towns, cemeteries, and the remains of prisons.

As a teenager in the 1970s, I never thought much about World War II. My history teachers, pressed to teach too much material in too little time, never discussed war beyond the major figures and battles. In the 1960s and 1970s, discussion centered on the latest newsreels on television from Vietnam. The only war I was familiar with was the Vietnam War—because my father was involved in it.

While my father was away fighting in that war, my mother tried to keep life as normal as possible for my brothers and me. We moved to Pennsylvania to be near family until my father returned from Vietnam. An uncle of mine, Lawrence Pifer, stepped forward to act as a surrogate father to three "fatherless" children.

My uncle is a sturdy, stoic Pennsylvania German. He told me he had fought in a war—World War II. He didn't know how lonely it felt to be a child with a father fighting a war on the other side of the world, but he knew what it was like to be a warrior. Then he told me he had even been a prisoner in Germany! Slowly, little bits and pieces of information came out. He laughed as I grimaced at the stories about the food he ate in POW camp. Surprisingly, I never worried about my father becoming a prisoner; the possibility of his death weighed more heavily on my mind. There was nothing my uncle could do to protect my father or his own son, but his solid, comforting presence made a difficult time better for me. I was lucky; my father came back from Vietnam. He later retired after twenty years in the U.S. Air Force. My cousin Larry also returned unscathed from service in Vietnam.

The relationship I had with my uncle strengthened as I became an adult. When we saw each other during family vacations, he shared more and more stories about his experiences in German POW camps. In the 1980s, he began to travel to squadron get-togethers and reunions of Ex-American Prisoners of War. After my uncle retired to Florida, he joined an American group of former POWs that met twice a month at the Gainesville, Florida, Veterans' Hospital.

While on a visit to Florida, I was introduced by my uncle to the chaplain, who led the group, and a couple of other members. After attending these sessions for a while, my uncle appeared to be even more eager to share his story with me. So I asked if he would allow me to interview him. When he agreed, we made plans to get together in January 1998 and visit the National Prisoner of War Museum in Andersonville, Georgia, site of a Civil War prisoner-of-war camp.

At that time, the Andersonville National Historic Site (NHS) museum was in a rather small, humble building in the park. A joint effort of federal, state, and local governments, and the enthusiastic help of veterans organizations, made it possible to build a new multimillion-dollar museum, which was to be completed in April 1998. When we visited that January, however, we saw a small museum and toured the NHS cemetery. For me, it was a poignant and memorable experience because not until I viewed photograph after photograph of Americans as prisoners of war did I realize that my uncle had not been alone. As long as there is conflict in this world, I realized, there would be prisoners of war.

Upon returning to Florida, my uncle and I sat down at his kitchen table, and for three days we recorded his memories on tape. As we read through his documents and maps, I took copious notes. We talked late into the night, and my aunt made sure we had plenty of coffee and food to keep up our strength. Afterward, I returned to Colorado to transcribe the tapes and organize my notes.

As I began to write, I shared my uncle's story with the Friday Afternoon Writing Group, a small group of writers who met in Littleton to critique each other's work. Two members of the group, World War II navy veterans Robert Poduska and Charles Kuhl, were writing their stories for their families, and they encouraged my effort and provided helpful criticism. At the same time, I expanded my search to military and American Red Cross records. I made numerous phone calls to my uncle to double-check facts and listen to more stories.

In November 1998, I flew to England to visit the Royal Air Force Museum at Hendon, near London, to view the extensive collection of WWII aircraft there. Returning to Colorado invigorated, I worked toward the goal of completing the manuscript by my uncle's August birthday. In August 1999, I proudly presented a bound copy to him. But the story was not over. I thought it was worth sharing with others beyond our family circle. It deserved a wider audience, but I was uncertain how to proceed.

It was not until two years later that I had an opportunity to return to Andersonville, Georgia, to see the new POW museum. In January 2000, my uncle and I toured the museum and its collection facilities with superintendent Fred Boyles and curator Eric Reinert. The museum's architect, Carla McConnell, had designed the new building to resemble a prison, down to the steel gates and narrow walkway that forced visitors to pass single file or in pairs as so many prisoners had to do when they entered prisons around the world. Chief Ranger Fred Sanchez and his interpreters superbly utilized the collections, making the most of mixed media, videotaped interviews of ex-prisoners, and the architecture of the building to interpret prisoner-of-war experiences from the American Revolution through Desert Storm.

At the end of our journey through the museum exhibits, my uncle and I passed through a pair of glass double doors to a courtyard. In the center of the courtyard was artist Donna Dobberfuhl's brick and bronze sculpture dedicated to all prisoners of war. The relief is composed of three large brick panels depicting twenty-five figures in a state of considerable suffering. The piece dwarfs all its surroundings. Standing in front of the relief, in bronze, a lone figure grasps and clutches, but does not manage to capture, the water that pours over his hands and through his fingers into a stream. Gaunt and haggard, the bronze figure and his shadowy fellow prisoners depict a combination of emotions—hardship, thanksgiving, and survival.

As I gazed through the lens of my camera, tears welled and spilled at the sight of my uncle near the bronze figure in front of the relief. The story that Technical Sergeant Lawrence I. Pifer had shared with me about his prisoner-of-war experiences was not someone else's memory—it was his alone. The hardships endured and the fight to survive was *his* battle. The men who struggled to survive in prison camps were real people, not characters in books or numbers in military reports. They cried real tears, fought real fears, and survived real ordeals.

When my cousin Donna Kadish used the first draft of my manuscript in her sixth-grade history curriculum, her students were enthralled and surprised to learn that their grandfathers or other family members had participated in the same war. They wanted to learn more about their elders, and if they did, I was sure that my uncle's story could be a valuable addition to any history curriculum, whether middle school or university level. If young children were interested in the story, perhaps others would be as well. I was determined to get my uncle's story published. The result is *Our Last Mission*, which became an all-consuming project that nagged at me until all other projects were pushed aside.

Finally, here it is—the story of one very real man who endured the trials of war to survive and tell his tale.

OUR LAST MISSION

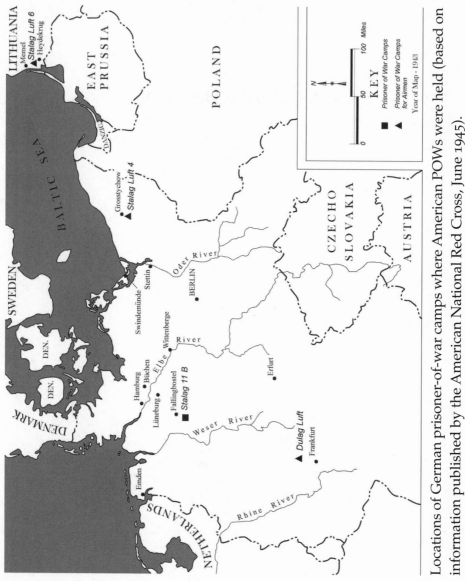

Locations of German prisoner-of-war camps where American POWs were held (based on information published by the American National Red Cross, June 1945).

CHAPTER ONE

THE EARLY YEARS

Excited and keyed up about their target, the invincible young crews were so busy with their individual jobs there was no time to think about what the future might bring. The drone of the bees grew and grew, breaking the stillness of the night. In the skies over Horham, England, green, blue, amber, and red lights flashed so quickly that one had to stand and stare intently to catch brief flashes in the darkness. Then suddenly the swarm of planes united into a force that could attack all who stood in their path with precision and the deadly sting of their bombs.

As the B-17 bombers moved into formation over England, communication ceased. The ten men inside each of the "Flying Fortresses" readied themselves for the battle ahead. Their mission on March 3, 1944, lay deep inside Germany. Their target was Berlin. No one to date had reached the inner sanctum of Hitler's kingdom, but today the mighty Eighth Air Force was determined to drop a few bombs for the Führer to contemplate.

The morning hung heavy with cloud cover. Pilots appreciated cloud cover when hiding from their enemy, but for bombardiers a clear view or at least breaks in the clouds helped to identify landmarks and targets. Static on the radio broke through the thoughts of the men inside *Slightly Dangerous* as they approached land somewhere near Rostock in northern Germany. Due to problems with visibility, English ground commanders diverted the bombers away from their intended target. The formation turned and bombed their second directive, Denmark, and the swarm headed back to base. On March 4th, the bombers of the Eighth Air Force would strike Berlin with a vengeance that won the Eighth Air Force a Distinguished Unit Citation. For one young American who signed on with the Army Air Corps, the mightiness of his bombardment group could not protect him.

The radio operator and ball-turret gunner of the *Slightly Dangerous* crew was Lawrence Pifer, a twenty-one-year-old from Pennsylvania. Born on a sultry August day in 1922, Lawrence Ivan Pifer was the second child and only son of Ruth and Ivan Pifer. Ruth's sudden death after an illness left her husband to raise a young daughter and a two-year-old son. Ivan could not deal with the responsibility and the two children were shuffled from relative to relative until he remarried when Larry was nine. The youngster and his sister, Helen, moved in with the newlyweds who lived on a rented farm near his paternal grandparents in the rolling hills of Jefferson County in central Pennsylvania. Larry's years with his aunt and then with his grandparents were nurturing, but that would change with the arrival of his stepmother.

Even though he was only nine and small for his age, Larry took on most of the farming chores. In the mornings, the boy headed to the barn to begin them as his father left for work in the bituminous coal mines that dotted the area. A belt of bituminous coal ran from West Virginia into southwestern Pennsylvania and petered out in the hills of Jefferson and Clearfield counties. Early farmers had entered the area and waged war on the thick blanket of trees that covered the rolling hills, eventually clearing enough farmland to support their families. Later speculators, engineers, and miners moved in to disembowel the earth, drawing out ton after ton of the black coal that fueled homes, trains, and steel and manufacturing plants.

The ten-acre farm Ivan rented for his family was large enough for a couple of cows and some chickens and ducks and for a large garden, which fed the family. After a day at school, Larry would return home to finish his remaining chores. When he refused to call his new stepmother "Mother," she took pleasure in finding fault with his work and doling out the punishment she felt he deserved. Wherever they were on the farm and whatever she could find to use on the youngster, whether it was a strap or piece of wood, the stepmother was relentless in her assaults on the boy, who took his punishment without tears or expression. The more stoic the face he wore, the worse the beating was, but Larry could not nor would not let her succeed in breaking him.

Helen, his sister, faced her share of the torment also. When she did not complete her chores in the allotted time, the teenager might be forced to wear the same dirty clothes to school for several days. It was humiliating for the freshman girl to be seen in such a state. The children's father never intervened on their behalf and they had no one to turn to. Their stepmother did not allow the children to see their grandparents, but whenever possible Helen and Larry stole away through the woods to visit them. Worried about getting in more trouble for seeing their grandparents and not wanting to worry them, Larry and Helen did not tell about the mental and physical abuse they received at home at the hands of their stepmother.

Then, after suffering for three years and finally fed up with it, Larry gave his father an ultimatum. The first rays of the morning sun were finding their way into the kitchen when Larry entered to find his father eating his breakfast alone. He seized the opportunity and demanded that either "she" went or he did.

Ivan looked up from his plate and fastened his eyes on the youngster. Larry did not flinch or drop his eyes, but stood his ground. The staredown did not last long. Without a word, Ivan resumed eating his meal. Larry turned and walked out the door. Later, as he crossed the barnyard and headed back to the house after completing his morning chores, Larry caught sight of his stepmother. He stopped and watched.

With angry strides, she marched down the lane clad in her coat and carrying her suitcase, and at the end of the lane she turned onto the road that headed into town. When she disappeared from sight, Larry turned toward the house and went inside to get ready for school. He never saw her again.

As Larry worked the farm and attended high school in Sykesville, he paid little attention to hints of growing unrest in Europe. Under Adolf Hitler's leadership, Germany's troops marched into Austria in March 1938. Hitler announced to the rest of the world the unification of Austria and Germany. Six months later, in September, in an attempt to garner peace for Europe, Britain and France signed the Munich Pact, allowing Germany to take over the Sudetenland, an area of Czechoslovakia largely inhabited by German-speaking citizens.[1] Within months, despite the peace pact, Europe braced for war. At home in Pennsylvania, Larry was only interested in what was going on in his life.

Graduated from high school and tired of the countless arguments with his father, Larry felt it was time to strike out on his own. It was late July 1941 when Larry and his cousin, Bob Lansberry, hitchhiked to New York. Larry's sister had moved to Niagara Falls to find a job in one of the city's manufacturing plants. Military enlistment had depleted the number of male workers and plants were hiring women to fill vacant jobs. "Come to New York," Helen said. And so he did.

Standing in line after line at plant after plant, Larry and Bob sought jobs. It was the same old story over and over again. Larry

Looking for work. Larry Pifer and Bob Lansberry on bridge near Mineral Springs, Pennsylvania, July 1941. Courtesy of Lawrence Pifer.

was told he was too young at seventeen to be hired. He should come back when he was twenty-one. When Bob found work, Larry returned to Sykesville.

However, he did not stay long; he just had to get out of Sykesville. Setting out with a group of friends who were also looking for jobs, Larry hitchhiked around Pennsylvania, first to a steel mill in Sharon, then to a railroad yard in Altoona, and eventually to York. As each of his buddies was hired, Larry grew discouraged. Turning to Larry, managers would tell him to move along and return when he was older.

After an unsuccessful job-hunting trip to Tennessee, a frustrated Larry still itching to travel, headed north again to Cincinnati, where he hired on with a firm that sold magazine subscriptions across the state of Ohio. The idea of traveling and making money appealed to him. However, he soon became discouraged with the pittance he actually made from selling subscriptions. Then, while in Cleveland, he saw a for-hire sign in the window of a Goodyear Tire store and went in to inquire. Larry's days of selling magazines were over! He had a job repairing and changing tires.

In Europe, a great war escalated and America's allies begged for assistance. President Roosevelt and a reluctant Congress moved toward military preparedness. A tense dance began between Japan and the United States as the Japanese moved into Manchuria and Southeast Asia, freezing out American and other foreign business interests. Roosevelt recalled our German, Italian, and Japanese ambassadors and froze those countries' funds that were in U.S. banks. Congress enacted embargos when the Rome-Berlin-Tokyo axis formed. American citizens generally felt that the war was "over there" and followed their day-to-day routines.

Then in December of 1941, after the horrendous Japanese attack on Pearl Harbor that killed over two thousand servicemen and civilians, American citizens dramatically changed their opinion. The United States military sent out a general call for all young men to enlist and assist America and its Allies in the great war. In August 1941, by a single vote, the House of Representatives had extended the draft law. After the bombing of Pearl Harbor, even though there was a rash of enlistments, the numbers did not meet the current demands made by America's military leaders. The military instituted the draft.

In the Cleveland Good Year store where Larry worked, married men, some with children, were called up. Larry, young, strong, healthy, and single, felt a growing unease, even a sense of guilt.

The sun glinted off the glass of the storefronts along Euclid Avenue as Larry made his way back from lunch to the tire store. He was satisfied with his life. He had a nice room, money in his pockets, and no worries to speak of. Trees were leafing and flowers beginning to bloom. Winter was over and spring was at hand. Then he caught sight of the man.

Larry glanced across the street and saw a large placard outside the post office proclaiming "Uncle Sam Wants You!" Larry swore that Uncle Sam's eyes followed him and the pointing finger bore into his backside as he hurried up the street. He turned to look again. Uncle Sam's pointing finger beckoned. The penetrating eyes of the stern gray-haired gent in white tophat drew Larry back down the street and into the post office. He succumbed. Lawrence Ivan Pifer enlisted in the United States Army Air Corps on May 22, 1942.

CHAPTER TWO

BASIC TRAINING

Because Larry was underage, the Army Air Corps sent a handful of forms to his father in Pennsylvania to notify him of Larry's intent to enlist. When Ivan signed and returned the papers, Larry took the test for entrance into the Army Air Corps and passed.

After a quick weekend visit home to central Pennsylvania, Larry traveled by train to Fort Benjamin Harrison, near Indianapolis, where he was sworn into the service. Within minutes of the ceremony, the new enlistees received fatigues and were directed to a waiting train. They were herded aboard and headed for basic training at Keesler Army Air Base in Biloxi, Mississippi. When alighting at the railway station in Biloxi, a sergeant directed the new arrivals to line up in formation. A captain in command proclaimed, "You are in the Army Air Corps now! Let's see you try to get out." The reality of the situation hit the young recruits. Taking orders had begun!

The recruits were assigned serial numbers and ranks. All men were identified by their surname. Larry soon learned to answer quickly when someone bellowed "Pifer!"

Drill sergeants kept the young recruits busy day and night. They had little time to themselves and the training period passed quickly. After years of working on a farm, Pifer's body was lean and muscular. He liked the looks of his five foot five inch frame in the olive-drab uniform. His unruly curly brown hair would have caused a problem with his hat, but it was closely shorn and the cap fit nicely to his head. When he studied his brown eyes in the mirror, Pifer thought he looked more mature and was a pretty good-looking son of a gun in his army uniform. Not all recruits were as physically fit as Larry and they suffered in the sweltering summer heat in Biloxi. Pounds were lost and muscles grew as the weeks passed until graduation from basic training.

After his six-week stint in basic training, Pifer hoped to be assigned to the artillery school for bombers' crews. Volunteers were allowed to choose a specific skill for training, while most draftees did not get such an opportunity. When the draftees came pouring into the army, they appeared to be directly assigned to combat forces. Looking for every opportunity to travel, Larry had enlisted in the Air Corps with high hopes of soaring above the clouds. The prospect of flying excited the adventurous youth and he immediately put in for aerial gunnery.

After three days of strenuous tests and a variety of physical exams that were required for entrance into the gunnery program, a doctor congratulated Pifer for passing with flying colors and announced that the young recruit was qualified for radio training. Larry was dumbfounded. He tried to explain to the doctor that he knew nothing about radios, but knew a lot about guns from living on a farm and hunting. Ignoring this information, the doctor waved him away. Before he could find the right individual to complain to, Pifer was on a train west.

As the train lurched out of the station, Pifer figured he might as well make the best of it. After all, he had no choice. He was glad to be leaving the heat and humidity of Mississippi behind. After a series of stations and car changes, the uniformed men

Airman Lawrence I. Pifer, U.S. Army Air Corps graduation. Courtesy of Lawrence Pifer.

made their way to Sioux Falls, South Dakota, where they would train as radio operators for the Army Air Corps.

In Sioux Falls, the hot summer sun bleached the wheat fields surrounding the makeshift base at the edge of town. Sultry winds entered the open windows of the recruits' classroom during these miserable August days. The post's staff under commanding officer Colonel Narcisse L. Cote made sure the students were kept busy with lectures and physical training and soon they learned to ignore the heat and their surroundings.

The sixteen-week training course included lectures on the theory of radio operations and language, as well as maintenance and repairs of radio and code instruments. With films and diagrams, instructors taught potential operators to analyze circuits, build sets from tubes, transmitters, and receivers, and then tune their own equipment. They learned to use the long-distance radio equipment found in the many classroom laboratories. Once they knew the ins and outs of their equipment, it was time to learn International Morse Code.

In order to graduate, the men had to be able to receive and translate the code and, in one minute, send a sixteen-word response. At first learning the code and responding to it went slowly, but then the men caught the competitive spirit and raced in pounding the code on their brass keys. Pifer's finger flew. He found he was quite good at code training. However, in the basic training courses, he was floundering.

After failing the first three-week course, Pifer was summoned by a post officer. He explained that the only thing that kept Pifer from failing out completely was his code scores. After reviewing Pifer's file a few minutes, he glanced up and asked the young airman where he sat in his training class. Startled at such a question, Pifer responded, "At the back of the room, sir." When asked if he had trouble hearing the instructor, Pifer admitted it was difficult much of the time to hear the instructor at the front of the large laboratory classroom. The officer informed the young trainee he would now sit at the front of the classroom and he had only this three-week session to improve his grades or he would be out. Moving up front helped Pifer pass his training course with a much-improved score, but he had other worries on his mind.

Most of the men trained at Sioux Falls went to ground stations. An operator had to volunteer for flight duty and Pifer reported to sign up to fly, but he was worried that he might not get that opportunity. Rumors raced through camp that if an operator passed with sixteen words per minutes on his test, he would certainly be grounded. The idea was that the lower the score, the faster the radio operator. Those mastering faster technical abilities were placed in ground command centers around the world. Operators in those centers were bombarded with transmissions and had to learn to react quickly and forward information on to their superiors. It was imperative to keep lines open for that next vital piece of information. Speed and accuracy were of the utmost importance.

Not leaving anything to chance, Pifer intentionally slowed his speed to twenty words per minute. He knew he could do better but wanted the opportunity to be placed on a flight crew. He succeeded. Within a few days of his final tests, Pifer was assigned to bomber-crew training.

As the harsh winds and snows of November slashed at the base, the Army Air Corps presented Pifer with his certificate for radio operators and mechanics and his Army Air Forces Technical School yearbook. He got orders to report to radio operations training and aerial gunnery school in Harlingen, Texas.

Harlingen, near Brownsville in the southernmost tip of Texas, was close to the border of Mexico. During an unusually warm winter in Texas—or maybe it seemed that way after South Dakota's bitterly cold winds—Pifer shed his parka and

SUSTINEO ALAS

ARMY AIR FORCES TECHNICAL SCHOOL

SIOUX FALLS, SOUTH DAKOTA

Cover of AAF Technical School Yearbook, Sioux Falls, South Dakota, 1942. Courtesy of Lawrence Pifer.

headed back to the classroom. Even though they had mastered the radio, Pifer and the other trainees practiced daily their skills in the mechanics and language of the radio. When they weren't in classrooms at the radios, they participated in field gunnery training at a shooting range in the desert.

During their first day of field training, Pifer and his group reported for an introductory course on the mechanics of shooting. A line of olive-drab uniforms formed at the skeet (clay pigeon) range and waited for direction. The drill sergeant asked who would like to go first. Pifer glanced over at Tony Sylvester, who had been a policeman in Columbus, Ohio, half expecting him to step forward. When no one volunteered, the instructor motioned for Pifer to step forward.

Never having been on a skeet range and seeing nothing around him to shoot at, a puzzled Pifer took the gun. The drill instructor directed Pifer to ready himself, yell "Pull" when ready, and shoot. Doing as he was told, Pifer was startled when he saw the clay pigeon shoot into the air, but he was able to take it out with one shot. The sergeant stared at him for a minute and said that was a lucky shot. Moving Pifer down the line from station to station, the instructor engaged in a shooting competition with the trainee. After completing the drill, a stunned Pifer realized he had beaten the instructor and a warm glow grew inside until he turned to see the sergeant glaring at him. "Where did you learn to shoot?" he barked. When Pifer replied on the farm in Pennsylvania, the instructor cocked his eyebrow and then shook his head. From then on, the two were in constant competitions, sometimes remaining after shooting practice to take each other on. Pifer never lost.

Gunnery school included classroom studies, shooting-range drills, and aerial gunnery training. In aerial gunnery training, two men—a pilot and a gunner—flew in an advance trainer, a Douglas AT6. The gunner sat with his back to the pilot and in front of a gun that slid to and fro on a track. The gunner was able to shoot only his thirty-caliber training gun to either side or to the rear. No chance of spinning around and shooting his pilot.

During target practice, a second plane trailing a target, or sleeve, flew at varying distances from the AT6. Since there were several training planes assigned to a target, it was necessary for each gunner to be assigned different colored ammunition. The bullets were tipped in paint of various colors so that when they tore through the sleeve paint stained the fabric. At the end of a four-hour training period, sleeves were collected and shots counted. A gunner received points according to how many times he hit his target. In order to graduate from the course, a trainee had to attain a set number of points that was assigned by the army.

Ground classes covered many topics. Trainees learned the theory of gunnery and air combat, including trajectory. Each man's ability to name the parts of the gun and be familiar with their functions was of utmost importance. The men learned to assemble, disassemble, and reassemble a gun in an allotted time. In addition, it was crucial for students to be able to distinguish enemy aircraft in a matter of seconds. Like schoolchildren learning math functions, the men practiced with flashcards of enemy and Allied aircraft over and over again until each student mastered the details of the world's airships. At this point, the men did not know if they were to be stationed in the Pacific or in Europe, so they learned to identify enemy and friendly aircraft from the East to the West.

Each weekday, trainees attended school and participated in aerial gunnery training. Every day at 6 A.M., Pifer awoke to reveille, dressed, and made his bed in six minutes. Then it was out for a one-mile run before breakfast, later in the evening a second mile was put in. After their run, the men had six minutes to shower and dress for breakfast. At the mess hall, Pifer and his buddies moved through the chow line and joined tray-bearing lines that led to a sergeant who directed them to a table. Lines of men, standing straight as ramrods, waited next to their seats until ordered to sit. Trays clattered onto the tabletops and men sat at attention until the order came to eat. Six minutes later, whether they were finished or not, orders were given to clear out. During childhood, Pifer had mastered the art of eating in a fraction of a minute so he could get away from his stepmother and back to his chores. He reckoned she had trained him well for the army life.

From the mess hall, streaming lines headed to classrooms or hangars. Often, Saturdays entailed parades and inspections. Sundays were days of rest and allowed each man time to polish his boots, check uniforms, write letters home, or relax. Pifer learned to play ping-pong and perfected his game of pool at the day room on base. Then their week began all over again. Once in awhile, they were given a reprieve and day passes were issued.

With one-day passes in hand, airmen crossed the border into Mexico to visit the small village of Matamoros. It was Pifer's first glimpse at another culture, as it was for many of the recruits. The bronze-skinned and raven-haired beauties fascinated the American servicemen. The soft pink and dirty orange adobe buildings, the color of the desert, provided the perfect backdrop to the brightly colored rugs and clothes of the peasants. Strangely named beers and spicy bean dishes tested their palates. Pifer's time away from the base was never long enough to suit him. All too soon, someone yelled that it was time to head back to base.

Not soon enough, it seemed to the trainees who were anxious to get into battle, final tests were taken and graduation came. On January 2, 1943, Pifer received his Certificate of Proficiency. Within days, he was flown to Salt Lake City to wait for assignment to a flight crew.

SUBJECT	HRS.	PCT.
ORIENTATION	2	
DESCRIPTION & NOMENCLATURE	27	
SHOTGUN .30 CAL.		
.22 CAL. .50 CAL.		
SIGHTS	3	
RING & BEAD TELESCOPIC		
REFLECTOR COMPENSATING		
SIGHTING & HARMONIZATION	12	
BALLISTICS	3	
AIRCRAFT RECOGNITION	11	
RANGE ESTIMATION	4	
OXYGEN EQUIPMENT &		
PRESSURE CHAMBER	5	
NAVAL RECOGNITION	5	
TACTICS	4	
TURRET DRILL	20	
TURRET MAINTENANCE	15	
CODE & VISUAL SIGNAL	15	
FIRING	80	

Malfunct.   30 Cal. 33 Rds.
              50 Cal. 83 Rds.
.22 Cal.   667 Rds.
Shotgun   333 Rds.
Gr. to Gr. 30 Cal.
Turret   300 Rds.
Hand-held   200 Rds.
Gr. to Gr. 50 Cal.
Turret   150 Rds.
Hand-held   100 Rds.
Air to Air 30 Cal.   800 Rds.

MILITARY TRAINING & ATHLETICS	40	
REVIEW	4	
TOTAL	**250**	

REMARKS:

EXPLANATION OF GRADES S-SATISFACTORY
U-UNSATISFACTORY   E-EXEMPTED
ALL GRADES SATISFACTORY
UNLESS OTHERWISE INDICATED

Certificate of Proficiency and grade report, Harlingen Army Gunnery
School, Harlingen, Texas, January 1943. Courtesy of Lawrence Pifer.

Boeing B-17, The Flying Fortress. Author's collection.

Salt Lake City was an army staging area for trained crewmen. Drill sergeants kept the men busy with fifteen-mile marches while in full field packs; they entailed running up the hill to the capitol, then back to their quarters. Pifer felt as if he were back in basic training. By mid-January, a commander assigned Pifer as an assistant radio operator to a B-17 crew and sent him off to Gowen Air Field in Boise, Idaho, to join up with his crew.

Upon arrival in Boise, Pifer learned that the film star Jimmy Stewart was a pilot in his squadron. The idea of seeing a real live film star thrilled Pifer, but he never did catch a glimpse of Stewart, who was kept busy with film publicity for the war effort. Due to the efforts of Stewart and other actors, the Army Air Corps was introduced in short newsclips to moviegoers across the country.

During World War I, the introduction of the airplane in combat hinted at its eventual role in future military campaigns. In 1917, Germany created the much-feared Gotha, the first successful heavy bomber. At the end of the war, the heavy bomber aircraft evolved to increase its flying range and carry heavier bombloads. With the introduction of the German bomber, the prospect of planes carrying bombs deep into enemy territory to destroy cities and industrial centers caused much consternation in governments around the world. Military heads in Italy, England, and the United States foresaw the future of air military campaigns, but their governments did not necessarily agree with them. The Italian government chose to listen to its commanding general Guilio Douhet, but subsequent predictions by British Air Marshal Sir Hugh Trenchard and U.S. General William "Billy" Mitchell were used against them.[1] Disciples of Mitchell, who by the 1920s was recognized as the father of American military aviation, persisted and a small force of long-range strategic bombers had been built in the early 1930s for the United States Army.

Lawrence Pifer's military pass for Gowen Field, Boise, Idaho, January 1943. Courtesy of Lawrence Pifer.

One of America's earliest bombers was the Boeing B-17 Flying Fortress, which boasted a two-thousand-mile range. At one hundred feet long and over thirty tons, the B-17 was the largest of the heavy bombers. On a typical mission, the bombload was four to five thousand pounds. During battle, even after receiving heavy damage, many a fortress safely carried its crew to home port. Crews affectionately named their planes and painted pictures, generally of pinup girls, on the noses of them.

During Pifer's first training flight on the B-17 over Idaho, a trainer tested him and the radio operator. Under the watchful eyes of the trainer, each operator tuned his radio, called the ground station, and logged on in Morse code. As Pifer's fingers flew, the startled trainer asked him what speed he achieved in school. When Pifer replied twenty words per minute, the trainer asked him what he was doing as an assistant. The next day, first radio operator Pifer was assigned to a new crew under the command of Lieutenant William Slabotny.

By March, Slabotny's crew was headed to Walla Walla, Washington, for the second phase of their training, an intensive course that would tax the limits of each and every man. Pifer crammed his military pass for Gowen Field into the back of his wallet and prepared to head to Walla Walla.

Training in Walla Walla was grueling. Days were spent in the air or on the ground going through drills, with little time for rest or sustenance. One-hour periods for food or sleep were given periodically throughout the day and into night. At one point, Pifer was barely awake as two of his crew members led him to the plane for their next "mission."

Bomb crewmen tended to be short in stature, because of the low ceiling of the bomber and its cramped quarters. The Army Air Corps set height restrictions for bomber crew members with the maximum height being approximately five and a half feet. The ball turret was so confining that the gunner needed to be even shorter than the rest of the crew. Despite the cramped quarters inside the bomber, the doorway into the plane was quite a distance from the ground. The men learned to jump up to grab the handles on either side of the opening and pull themselves in quickly. There were no steps to boost them inside. Their first tries at pulling themselves into the plane were cause for laughter. A few of the men hit the tarmac on their backsides. Swinging up into the opening strengthened their arm muscles and before long they literally flew through the hole.

Once inside the opening at the nose of the B-17, the ten-man crew moved into their respective positions. The nose gunner-bombardier was the first into his position in the glass nose of the plane. The rest of the men moved to the back of the plane. The position nearest the doorway was that of the pilot and copilot. They crawled into place behind a glittering board of lights, switches, and hand controls. The aft men gingerly walked to the back on a narrow strip of metal masquerading as a walkway. It was like walking on an acrobat's balancing beam. Pifer joined the aft men as they headed to their respective positions.

Passing the position of the flight engineer, who also manned the upper-turret guns, the aft men entered the bomb bay with its dismantled training dummies. Just behind the bomb bay, Pifer and his assistant radio operator slid into their positions in front of the red, yellow, and blue knobs of the radio and near enough to their guns to spring into action during combat. Behind them, two waist gunners manned fifty-caliber machine guns on either side of the plane and the tailgunner held his position in the rear with two guns. Each crew member was a specialist of some sort, and all were trained to perform other jobs in the aircraft during combat.

Slabotny's crew flew a bomber from Walla Walla to Madras, Oregon, southwest of Walla Walla, for yet another stint of training. For thirty days, the men were without a ground crew to service their plane. Each crew member maintained and operated his component function in the plane as part of ongoing training. Flying maneuvers included bombing and navigation runs. Touch-and-go landings called "shooting landings," were practiced. The wheels barely touched the ground before they lifted off once again. Other landings involved taxiing down the runway, turning and taking off again. Finally, it was time for them to receive their combat bomber.

The army ferried the crewmen to Salina, Kansas, to pick up their new bomber for combat. On the flight back to Washington, all four engines of the B-17 developed oil leaks and they touched down in Great Falls, Montana, for repairs. When they got back to Walla Walla, the commander announced to the mortified crew that four of the ten men would remain at the training school as instructors. The army needed instructors to teach the swelling numbers of recruits in the Air Corps. It took the top two students from each graduating class and assigned them to the training school. The first pilot, Slabotny; the assistant flight engineer; assistant radio operator; and Pifer, as first radio operator, were to remain at Walla Walla. Replacements would join the bomber and the rest of Slabotny's crew.

CHAPTER THREE

ARMY INSTRUCTOR

In Pennsylvania, the local newspaper, the *Clearfield Progress*, reported that Staff Sergeant Larry Pifer, a graduate of Radio School at Sioux Falls, South Dakota, and Aerial Gunnery School at Harlingen, Texas, was now stationed at Walla Walla, Washington, as a radio operator and gunner instructor aboard a B-17, the Flying Fortress of the United States Army Air Corps. Even hearing that his picture and name were in the newspaper did not cheer up the unhappy airman.

A disappointed Pifer watched as his buddies in their B-17 bomber joined the formation in the sky above the town of Walla Walla. His throat clutched as he watched the planes become a speck in the sky before they disappeared. Pifer was angry at being left behind. "I didn't enlist to train other soldiers," he moaned. He wanted to fly in combat. He wanted a break from the army. He hadn't seen his family in months. Pifer stood and stared at the now empty sky and vowed that he would do whatever he could to get into combat.

Anger seethed in Lieutenant Slabotny at the unfairness of the situation. His men should have been with the formation. Glancing at the remaining men in his crew, Slabotny turned and with determination marched to the command office to petition a

S/Sgt. Lawrence Pifer in flight suit. Photograph taken in Redmond, Oregon, in March 1943 while Pifer was stationed at Walla Walla, Washington. Courtesy of Lawrence Pifer.

fifteen-day furlough for the grounded four. When their passes came through, Pifer and his buddies readied their bags and headed to the train station.

When Larry got to Pennsylvania, the countryside had responded to the long warm days of June and burst forth in lush shades of green. Summer flowers bloomed in the gardens. Farmers' crops were in. Green rows stretched across the hills of central Pennsylvania. Much of his furlough time, Larry ate. Family and friends invited the young airman to dinner or on picnics and Larry relished all the home-cooked meals after mess-hall meals. On one of Helen's visits, Ivan suggested that they take this opportunity to get a family photograph. The brother and sister were surprised when their father proposed a professional photographer and quickly agreed.

Away from the day-to-day routine and structure of army life, Larry's anger over being grounded dissolved, but he could not help but wonder what would happen to the rest of the crew. On paper, the four left behind were a crew, but since it took ten to fly a plane, the chances of the crew remaining together were slim. Would they fill in empty positions on other flight crews or be assigned four more members? Instead of fretting about further breakup of the crew during his short furlough, Larry threw himself into activity and decided to find out when he got back to Walla Walla. All too soon, he found himself on a train full of uniformed men headed west.

Back at the training base, Pifer and his assistant flight engineer shared their frustration over the breakup of the crew and decided that between the two of them they would devise a plan to get sent to the front. One night while sitting over a few drinks at a bar in Walla Walla, Pifer and his buddy pledged with bravado to stay drunk until they were fired as instructors. Surely, their commanders would send them to war as punishment.

Pifer family photograph taken in June 1943. From left to right, Lawrence, Ivan, Helen. Courtesy of Lawrence Pifer.

Since he never was much of a drinker, it didn't take much alcohol for Pifer to get drunk. When his crew had gone out on a Friday or Saturday night to the local bars, the guys tormented Pifer about his "sissy" cola drinks. They claimed he wasn't man enough to drink the hard stuff, but he laughed and stuck with his soda pop. Now Pifer found that after a couple of alcoholic drinks, he was done in.

When Pifer staggered into the barracks in the morning, his pilot sent him to his bunk. After this happened three times, Pifer realized that every time he came in drunk and got sent to his quarters the trainer that he was to have flown crashed and all on board perished. If he had made the flight that day, he certainly would have died. Never one for religion, Pifer began to think that maybe someone, even God, had a plan for him after all. He wasn't meant to die yet. Foolishly, the young airman never considered the numbers of deaths racking up at the front. Bombers were going down. Ground troops suffered great casualties. Nevertheless, Pifer continued to pester his commanding officer for reassignment. He was ready to go to war.

In between training runs and classroom lectures, the airmen found time for recreation on or off the base. Pifer and a friend, Daniel Aceita, met at the pool in town to swim as often as possible. The two were surprised one day when they arrived to see a handsome couple taking laps in the pool. Pifer and Aceita did not remember seeing this particular couple there before. Then Aceita recognized them.

Alan Ladd and his wife and agent, Sue Carol, were in Walla Walla filming a movie. After a decade of small parts in B movies, the blue-eyed blond finally came to fame in 1942. At five foot six, Ladd's height hampered his career, but when fate paired him with the diminutive Veronica Lake in *This Gun for Hire*, he achieved stardom. After completing a couple of short takes, *Hollywood in Uniform* and *Skirmish on the Home Front*, for the war effort, Ladd was in Walla Walla making a movie portraying a World War II bombardier. When the young airmen struck up a conversation with the couple, Ladd invited them to come and see some of the filming. Pifer and Aceita eagerly accepted the offer and at the first chance made their way to the set near the edge of the base.

On the set, designers placed a cutaway of a B-17 bomber on sawhorses. The action "in the air" took place three feet off the ground. The airmen watched the actors "fly" their bomber into enemy territory over Europe. Ladd's character was a corporal and bombardier on the B-17's crew. The bombardier used maps and aerial photographs to determine when the bomber was over its target. Calculating the distance and timing for release of bomb payload, the bombardier pushed the button or pulled the lever to release the bombs. During most of the filming, Ladd wedged his small frame into the glass nose of the bomber behind a set of guns and near the instrument panel. When the script called for rough weather in combat, the cameraman jerked the camera up and down as the actors pretended to evade enemy fighters and bomb their targets.

After shooting for the day was completed, Alan and Sue Ladd took the time to meet with the two airmen at a local gathering spot in Walla Walla. Over the course of filming, the Ladds met Pifer and Aceita several times for drinks or a swim in the pool. For Pifer and Aceita, it was exciting to be swimming or having drinks with an actual movie star. In his letters to Aunt Helen and to his sister, Helen, Pifer gave an account of each of his meetings with the Ladds. Larry, the boy from small-town America, was finally experiencing some of the adventures he thought he would find in the army. More than ever, he was determined to get into battle. Then the door of opportunity opened.

One morning a messenger arrived to tell Pifer to report to the operations officer. As Pifer stood at attention, the officer sharply barked, "You sure you want to go to combat?" When Pifer responded with a resounding yes, the officer told him to check out three crews on base who had openings. He urged the radio operator to meet the crews, fly with them in training, and make a decision as to which crew he would like to fly with. Several days later, Pifer stood in front of the Crew Members' Board and ran his finger down the list until he came to the first one without a radio operator. He pinned his nametag to Lieutenant Melvin Dunham's crew. Then Pifer reported his decision to the operations officer, who sternly warned him that if he screwed up by being drunk or missing even one formation he would spend the rest of his days in the military as an instructor in Walla Walla.

With his heart racing, Pifer ran back to the barracks to tell his buddies. A group had congregated near the door and one yelled out to him to join them to go into town to celebrate their buddy's recent marriage. The bride and groom were waiting in town for them. After much persuasion by his friends, Pifer agreed to go only if they did not expect him to drink with them, except for a toast to the couple. He showered and got into his Class As and headed into town—not to drink, but to celebrate— or so he thought.

With a bottle of whisky in front of them and a pan of divinity supplied by the new bride, the airmen saluted and raised their shot glasses in a toast to the couple. The men savored the sweetness of the candy paired with the bitter whiskey, and they rose eagerly to make toast after toast to the newlyweds. Within a short time, they were all drunk, including Pifer!

When the bar refused to serve them any more liquor, the men and women decided to go bowling. On their way to the bowling alley, someone spied another bar and they went inside for just one more toast. As in most military towns, there seemed to be an abundance of drinking establishments. The celebrants found three bars on their way to the bowling alley, which of course they just had to enter. By the time Pifer and friends arrived at the bowling alley, they were sorely drunk. The proprietress, who had often challenged Pifer to a bowling contest, saw her chance to finally win. She challenged the drunk and he lost.

When morning came, Pifer awoke with a heavy head and wondered how in the world he got back to the barracks. As his head began to clear, he realized with horror that he had slept through skeet-range practice. "The commander will surely ground my ass," he thought bitterly.

Quickly, he ran to the infirmary and begged the clerk to put his name on the sick list. Patiently listening to the pleading sergeant's story, the medic acquiesced. Armed with an APC, or aspirin, for his aching head, Pifer staggered back to his quarters to sleep off his hangover. Realizing that he had narrowly escaped being grounded again, he pledged to himself to keep out of town and bars for the rest of his time at Walla Walla.

In late October of 1943, Aceita shook hands with his buddy, told him to write from the front, and waved goodbye as he saw Pifer off at the rail station. Staff Sergeant Pifer and a large group of airmen reported to a processing and overseas staging base in Herington, Kansas. Once processed in, Pifer met up with the rest of Lt. Melvin Dunham's crew. Dunham informed his crew that they would be flying to England as a replacement bomber.

The crew consisted of Lieutenants Melvin Dunham, pilot; Robert Renner, copilot; John Mathews, navigator; and Everett Lund, bombardier. The noncommissioned officers and gunnery crew included Sergeants Clarence Barstow, left waist gunner; Vincent Aiello, right waist gunner; Fred Bittner, tailgunner; Marvin Anderson, flight engineer and upper-turret gunner; Warren Thompson, assistant radio operator and gunner; and Lawrence Pifer, first radio operator. For final processing before leaving the States, the crew boarded another train that would take them to Camp Kilmer in New Jersey, where they would be assigned to Colonel Lacey's group heading to England. From New Jersey, they would take a ship to Great Britain.

At the dock, the men gazed up and up at the dull gray paint of the magnificent *Queen Elizabeth* berthed in the Hudson River, east of Manhattan. Equipped with wartime armament, the passenger streamliner barely hinted at her earlier passenger cruises on the oceans of the world. Only two civilian liners, the *Queen Elizabeth* and *Queen Mary*, were converted for military service. Their speed and maneuverability allowed them to evade enemy U-boats, travel the Atlantic alone, and deliver troops and equipment to points in Great Britain. On November 2, 1943, Pifer stood on *Elizabeth*'s deck and watched the New York skyline disappear. He was finally going into combat.

CHAPTER FOUR

INTO BATTLE

A fter docking in Scotland, trains took the new arrivals south to points along the eastern coast of England. Sgt. Pifer did not know what to expect. "No use worrying," he thought, and sank back in his seat to enjoy the Scottish countryside as it rushed by. He had never been overseas and he was fascinated by the snow-laden hills and glens of Scotland, where fat sheep blanketed in their thick woolen coats nibbled at any green they could find.

The train traveled through Scotland before entering England's hills, valleys, and forests. Due east of Cambridge and north of the coastal town of Ipswich, Lt. Dunham's crew disembarked in the picturesque country village, Horham, where the 95th Bombardment Group of the Eighth Air Force was now based. The 95th Bombardment Group had joined the Eighth Air Force in April 1943. The bombardment group flew its first mission with the Eighth Air Force on May 13, 1943, out of Framlingham, and it moved to Horham in June of the same year. By the time the 95th Bombardment Group flew its last mission in April of 1945, it had completed 320 runs and received three Distinguished Unit Citations. Forests and farmland surrounded the temporary installation at Horham. Pifer felt that he was at home.

Upon arrival at the base, Dunham's crew was assigned to the 335th Bombardment Squadron. Four squadrons formed a bomb group. In the 95th Bombardment Group, the squadrons included the 334th, 335th, 336th, and the 412nd. A squadron included approximately twenty-one planes. Due to casualties or repairs, the number of planes fluctuated. The squadron leader assigned the crew to a B-17 that they named *Slightly Dangerous*.

A cartoon picture of a pin-up girl with a resemblance to Lana Turner graced the nose of the aircraft. Many of the aircraft sported pictures of pin-up girls and cartoon animals. Above them, small bombs were painted in a row, designating how many missions the aircraft had completed. After twenty-five missions, a flight crew was eligible to return stateside.

Within a day or two of arriving, Lt. Dunham sought out Pifer. Dunham needed a ball-turret man and asked if Pifer was interested. The ball turret was a glass dome that hung under the belly of the B-17. The turret was fitted with a pair of fifty-caliber machine guns and it was a tight squeeze for a gunner to get into position behind them.

Located aft of the radio command center, the turret gunner dropped into the ball or globe from within the aircraft, pulling the hatch closed behind him. The hatch became the back of his seat. With elbows to his knees, the ball-turret gunner appeared to be almost in a fetal position in front of his guns. Surrounded by glass and hanging exposed to fighters, many gunners felt as though they were in a free fall. To get out of the ball turret, a gunner reached back to release the latch and then backed out into the belly of the plane.

Generally, assistant radio operators manned the ball turret, but in this case, Dunham's assistant radio man, Thompson, felt claustrophobic in the ball and asked the pilot for another gunner position in the plane. Pifer's height—five foot five—made him a perfect candidate for the station. Since being in the ball

The B-17 *Slightly Dangerous.* On top of the plane is Marvin D. Anderson, flight engineer. Pilot Melvin B. Dunham is in the lower right corner. To the left of Dunham is an unidentified grounds crewman. Horham, England, 1943. Courtesy of Lawrence Pifer.

did not bother him, he agreed to man the guns of the ball turret during battle.

Training flights over England allowed the new arrivals to become familiar with the English coastline, terrain, and the locations of cabled balloons near surrounding towns and cities. The British suspended balloons to deter German aircraft from bombing their communities. If the fighters flew in too low or too close, their wings became entangled in the cables and they crashed to the ground. American radio operators practiced the English signal language that they would use during their time there. Now it was time for their first mission.

On December 11, 1943, Dunham's crew flew off with a contingent from the Eighth Air Force for Emden. Located on the coast of Germany and northeast of the Netherlands, Emden housed a submarine pen. In the darkness over Horham, the planes lifted off one by one and fell into formation, lining up behind the colored light assigned to each squadron. As tailgunner, Bittner affixed a green-colored lens to the Aldis lantern located in the rear of the bomber. He flashed the light a couple of times to signal the plane that was just reaching altitude. Seeing the blinking light, the bomber flew into formation.

Adrenalin pumped through the veins of the rookie crewmen as they followed the orders issued by Dunham through the onboard intercom system.

All communication between the bombers ceased when they took to the air. Communication only resumed if there was a recall to base or an emergency. Inside each aircraft, the noise was deafening. Pifer thought it sounded like a jackhammer going full tilt inside a telephone booth. The intercom system attached to their headphones allowed the crew to talk to each other, but their conversation could not be detected outside the aircraft. Headphones and oxygen masks covered all but their eyes, which was actually a blessing because the inside temperature of the plane was frigid at high altitudes, often thirty, forty, even fifty degrees below zero. During the flight, a "halo" of ice particles formed around the fur trim of their soft leather helmets. Heated flight suits, nicknamed bunny suits, were plugged into outlets near each crew member's post. The plane's electrical power heated these suits. Even so, the crew members donned as much of their clothing as they could and still move freely. Over their bunny suits, they put on their coveted sheepskin-lined flying jackets and helmets. The electrical suits were notorious for shorting out and leaving their owners exposed to the elements. The leather jackets were practical, but had also become a flashy symbol of the daring flyer.

Pifer glanced over at his assistant, Thompson. Fear showed in their eyes and they looked away. Pifer listened intently for any communication from the pilot or the planes around them. He prayed he would not freeze in fear and let his crew down but would hold his own in battle. After practicing for so long, the crewmen anxiously waited for their first contact with the enemy and worried how they would react in actual combat.

Their breaths came fast and shallow, until the rhythm of their work calmed taut nerves. They speculated on what they would encounter first—Focke-Wulf 190s or Messerschmit fighters or flak. In the briefing, they were warned again about the dangers of enemy flak, short for the German word *Fliegerabwehrkanone*, which is actually debris from anti-aircraft cannon bursts.

The Germans did not necessarily care whether they hit the bombers with their flak, but focused on sending it up into concentrated areas, forcing the bombers to fly through it. Debris hitting the bombers punctured the shell of the craft or wings or was sucked into engines, causing many a bomber to crash.

Each wing of the bomber held approximately fourteen hundred gallons of fuel. The wings had the capability to self-seal; however, if a shell got into the tank and then exploded, the bomber became a fireball. Planes entering a stricken bomber's "prop wash" could be set into a spin and be pulled down with the falling craft. For the crew of *Slightly Dangerous*, this would be the first experience with flak in battle.

As *Slightly Dangerous* drew near the coastline of the Netherlands, the gunners manned their stations. Pifer crawled inside the ball turret and fastened his oxygen mask and turret headphone into place. Aiello and Barstow removed the hatches in front of their machine guns and a frigid blast of air filled the interior of the plane. Bittner kneeled and sat back on the seat pad in front of the two machine guns in the cramped tail section. He opened the hatch in front of his guns. Chances were, he would kneel in his crouched position for hours. Out of sight from the rest of the crew, it was a lonely place in times of battle. A religious man, Bittner used this time to kneel in prayer asking God to protect the crew and plane and carry them safely back to base.[1] Thompson stood by the upper single fifty-caliber gun. The bombardier and navigator protected the front of the plane and its nose with their guns.

In his hanging position inside the ball turret, Pifer saw the first of the ground fire coming straight at him. He knew that ground offenses were generally grouped into a battery of four guns. He saw the puff of smoke from the first gun and waited for the other three to follow. He breathed a sigh of relief when he realized that his plane was out of reach of the flak.

As he swung the ball turret around in looking for more flak or fighters, something caught his eye off to his left. His stomach lurched and he fought back the bile that rose in his mouth. Pifer stared in horror at a ball-turret gunner dangling by his boots from the smashed globe of a B-17. The airman was headless. The flak that had missed Pifer and *Slightly Dangerous* had found another target. Battling back the tears, Pifer spun his ball to and fro as more flak appeared. He was in combat and had no time to dwell on what he had seen.

Off to his right, Pifer saw a Focke-Wulf heading straight for his bomber. He watched as balls of fire shot toward him, but they fell short of their target. The ball turret rotated smoothly in his hands and he faced the Focke-Wulf for battle. The rat-a-tat-tat of the rounds from his guns roared in his ears and Pifer lost all sense of his plane and its crew above him. He was in a womb separated from the rest of the men. He fired and swung his ball around and fired some more.

The bombs were unleashed and Pifer watched them fall away before returning fire. Miraculously, pilots Dunham and Renner dodged their bomber through a heavy barrage of flak and pointed it back toward the North Sea and the safety of England. The commander of the operation sent out a general message to all the bombers to break formation. They were sitting ducks because of the amount of flak in the area. "Good luck, gentlemen. Get back the best way you can."

When the last of the flak bursts was behind them, the gunners slumped back to relax their tense muscles and then moved into their flight positions. Pifer climbed out of the ball turret and reclaimed his place in front of the radio. Within six hours, the crew was back on the ground in England and reporting for debriefing.

In the interrogation barracks, each man was offered a shot of whiskey to calm his nerves, toast the success of the mission, and honor lost comrades. Then they were invited to sit down to recount their battle experience. Everyone took a turn describing the battle, noting any land coordinates spied, and identifying any German fighters encountered during battle. Interrogators offered steaming coffee and doughnuts to those who waited for their chance to offer up any helpful information. As Pifer and his crew learned rather quickly, they must fly their mission, report their ordeal, and then try to forget about the death and destruction they left in their wake. They did not—could not— allow themselves to dwell on it. To survive with their sanity, the men of the bombardment groups had to will themselves to forget.

The glamour of battle soon wore off as the harsh realities of combat and a bomber's life became all too apparent. Rising at four in the morning, men crawled out of bed to dress in the bitter cold of their Quonset barracks and head to chow. Hot coffee seared their throats and they quickly swallowed their fried eggs, bacon, and toast. Running to the briefing room, they got their credentials checked by a guard and found a seat on a bench or stood around the room.

A film screen at the end of the room flashed pictures of maps, land coordinates, and enemy aircraft. Maps and photos lined the walls. A last cup of coffee was gulped. Then each squad ran to the hangars where ground crews readied the bombers for battle. Each man checked his parachute, ammunition, and guns. Everyone climbed aboard and soon the go-ahead signal was given. The bombers taxied to the runway and joined the formation at twelve thousand feet above the ground. When the air got thin, masks were donned. As land dropped away and water appeared below, gunners fired test shots to make sure they did not have a jammed gun before entering battle. "Enemy coast ahead!" someone yelled. They readied themselves and waited for the battle to ensue.

It was on their third mission that the rookie crew of *Slightly Dangerous* learned never to become too complacent. As the flying fortress lifted off from the field and entered formation, a top shaft sheared, causing engine number four to windmill. The shaft acted like a lance and impaled engine number one, which instantly feathered. Dunham shut it down. The deafening roar of the engines dropped a level when the engine shut off, and someone could be heard over the on-board sound system, swearing under his breath. Pifer glanced around at the other men and pondered the situation. Dunham's voice came over the internal intercom. "You want to about or keep in formation? It is up to you guys. We do it together or not at all." A chorus of "Let's go" followed his query.

Green lights continued to blink occasionally around them until all the planes were in formation. Today their destination was the shipyards in Bremen, Germany. It was December 16, 1943.

Despite the unanimous decision, tension was high. Pifer, who had a lot of confidence in his pilots, concentrated on his duties at the radio. After preparing emotionally for a mission, most crew members found it difficult to shut down their emotions and turn off the adrenaline rush. The crewmates of *Slightly Dangerous* focused on their roles in the B-17.

Shortly after releasing the bomb payload, the number four engine took a hit. With only two engines operating, the plane immediately plunged. When it began to lose altitude, Dunham yelled back to Pifer, "Get the hell out of the ball turret."

Lifting himself into the belly of the plane, Pifer saw waist-gunner Aiello coming toward him. He ducked his head and Aiello tossed something out the side door. Dunham had given orders to eject everything that was not attached to the plane to lighten their load. Frantically, the crew threw out ammunition, guns, radio equipment, armor plate—anything they could get loose from the interior of the plane went out the windows and hatches so that the plane had less to pull.

Dunham yelled for Pifer to get a QDM, or coordinate, anything from ground command. Pifer turned to see his assistant getting ready to toss the direction-finding station! Without it, they would not be able to determine which direction they were headed. Grabbing the piece of equipment from Thompson, he pointed to the units that could be thrown out. Pifer quickly set up the transmitter and switched from antennae to antennae, desperately trying to get a reading for his pilot.

Dunham shouted for everyone to prepare to crash into the sea. Rushing into the radio room, the crew lined up in bobsled fashion down the center behind Pifer at his station, which faced toward the bomb bay and cockpit. When Pifer turned away from his station, he realized there wasn't any room for him in the aisle. The only secure place left was his station. Quickly, he wrenched his seat from its bolts and threw it out the door. He saw it bounce off the side of the plane as he ducked his head back inside. With his back against the bulkhead under the radio table, he joined the others in puffing a cigarette that Lund, the bombardier, passed around. Pifer felt a little like a man having a last cigarette before dying at the hands of a firing squad. Except his death might be from a crash into the North Sea.

When the plane leveled off about ten feet above the water, Dunham radioed back to Pifer and asked if he could try again for a reading without leaving his safe zone. Peeking out from under the table, the radio operator could see that the dynamometer light was out, but pushing the plug in with his foot caused the light to glow. Reaching over the top of the table, he tapped out a request for a bearing. To his relief, a message came in and he forwarded it to Dunham. He sat back for further orders and within a few minutes Dunham called for another bearing. Before the tap-taps of the message were complete, others on the frequency broke in by holding down the button, a signal to let the operator know they had a bearing on his location.

Miraculously, *Slightly Dangerous* hovered over the water, saving the men from testing the seaworthiness of their emergency rafts. The crew marveled that the German fighters did not find them and send them into the ocean before they got to the coast of England. Routinely, the Germans sent out fighters after major battles to seek and destroy wounded Allied planes.

Perhaps they felt certain that the American bomber would go down without any assistance from them.

Every so often the props sliced the waves and a spray flew back over the plane. The two remaining engines fought to keep it in the air. Off the coast of England, the crew spied the white cliffs of Dover. They prayed Dunham would be able to get enough lift from the engines to clear the cliffs. With a roar, the plane rose up and over. Ground station personnel came over the frequency and directed the pilots to land at an emergency landing strip in nearby Bungay, a B-24 base.

Just as the wheels of *Slightly Dangerous* hit, the propeller flew off and neatly removed another engine and part of the tail. The plane fishtailed, but the pilot kept control as best he could until it stopped. They all exploded sighs of relief. It was the longest seven-hour mission they had experienced!

The flyers milled around slapping each other on the back and sent up cheers for their pilots. When the crew looked at their plane, they couldn't believe their eyes. Its ravaged body was pitted with holes from flak bursts. The skin of the bomber was dented by debris from the explosion of the engines and from the objects the men had thrown out, including the radio operator's chair. Aiello and Bittner laughed and marveled at Pifer's strength in yanking out his seat that was bolted to the floor of the plane. The radio operator's chair was anchored with four half-inch bolts. When the men eventually got back to their home base, several of the crew went out to another B-17 and tried to move the radio operator's chair. Two of them together could not even wiggle the chair. They agreed it was amazing what an adrenalin-charged man can do.

The crewmen reluctantly left their bomber behind and a Royal Air Force truck carried them back to base. It was two in the morning before they made it to debriefing and found that they were listed as missing in action! Their ground maintenance crew was glad to see them back safely. The flyers of *Slightly Dangerous* apologized to their ground crew chief for losing his plane. It was her forty-ninth mission. If the plane had completed only one more mission, the crew chief would have been sent back to the States. He waved them off and said he was simply relieved that they all had made it back safe and sound.

CHAPTER FIVE

SLIGHTLY DANGEROUS II

While Dunham's crew waited for a new aircraft, the damp cold of the English squalls wore on the their nerves. Storms and cloud cover grounded missions even before they had begun. The Army meteorologist would not even forecast more than three days ahead. During that winter, weather conditions only permitted five or six missions a month. The grounded air force tried to keep warm and busy while waiting for the weather to clear.

The corrugated metal huts that made up the base at Horham were freezing cold away from the portable potbelly stoves. Thankfully, there was plenty of coal to fuel the stoves. The eighteen men inside each hut kept the stove fired day and night. Nine bunks lined the sides of the hut, and above the head of each bed there was a shelf with hooks. The straw mattresses were lumpy and uncomfortable except when the men were exceptionally tired. At the foot of each bed, there was a trunk for each man's possessions.

At one end of the building, tables were available for writing letters, playing cards, or whatever else the men chose to do to while away the time. Airmen hung pictures of family, friends, and movie pin-ups along the walls to remind them of home.

On base, there were several recreational buildings. A small machine shop allowed the men to work on bicycles and build things like tables for their huts. A club where they could gather to play cards, games, or craps offered an outlet from the monotony of their sleeping barracks. Cooks and their assistants kept the mess hall and kitchen operating all day. Coffee was always available in large boilers on top of the portable stoves.

On Christmas Day, 1943, the cooks worked for hours preparing a feast. The line to the mess hall snaked for a quarter of a mile with four to five men across. Many put on a chipper front to hide homesickness. The cooks laid out a spread that was worth the wait. The formality of training camp was chucked as men filled their plates, sat with their buddies, and dug into their turkey with all the fixings.

Painfully stuffed, Pifer returned to his Quonset and wrote to Dan Aceita, his buddy in Walla Walla, Washington. In his letter, Larry complained of the boredom between missions. However, he had heard through the buzz around camp that a large offensive was brewing. He told Aceita not to envy him being in combat—it wasn't all that they thought it would be—and to be happy that he was an instructor and safe at his base in Walla Walla.

Larry gave an account of the good friends that he had lost in battle since his first mission. He expressed his helplessness and sorrow when he watched their planes go down right beside him during a mission. The only thing that Larry felt he could do to avenge his buddies was to go up the next day with the determination to shoot down the first "Nazi bastard" that he was close enough to take out of the sky. The young airman asked about his buddies at the training center in Washington and wished them all well.

A week after Christmas, on December 30, the crew of *Slightly Dangerous* flew toward Ludwigshafen, a manufacturing center on the western edge of Germany, in a loaner bomber. Until the crewmen received a replacement plane, they flew bombers not yet assigned to permanent crews. Flak followed them the entire way. The ball-turret gunner's eyes followed the bursts of flak by counting one, two, and three. "Damn," Pifer thought, "the fourth one is going to hit me."

Pifer spun the ball turret as fast as he could and the cannon glanced off, exploding near the waist-gunner's window. Barstow started screaming that he was hit. He slumped to the floor and another gunner raced to his machine gun. After the battle, worried crew members rushed to Barstow's side to see what they could do for him. Pifer and Bittner kneeled over the blanketed gunner and asked where he had been hit. Barstow raised his hand and showed them his bloodied left thumb. He excitedly told them he was going to put in for the Purple Heart! He had been injured in battle! His two colleagues were so mad at him they felt like throwing him out the door. Barstow had left his position and worried them sick over an injured thumb!

The day after their mission, the crew of *Slightly Dangerous* got their first forty-eight-hour pass. Larry Pifer, Fred Bittner, and Vince Aiello decided it was time to go to the city. They had heard about the sights of London and they could not think of a better place to ring in the New Year.

At the rail station in Horham, they stood on the platform with a throng of other airmen who had had the same idea. The train to London arrived with its aisles filled, but the passengers crammed together and made room for the airmen.

When the train arrived in London, Pifer and his buddies found themselves smack in the center of the city. Volunteers of the American Red Cross had a booth at the main train station and met arriving soldiers to assist them in finding hotel accommodations. With reservations set for that night, they stood in front of a map of the "tube," as the Brits referred to their subway system, and contemplated what to do next. Instead of getting onto the subway, they decided to walk the streets for a while and see the sights while it was still daylight.

The city's historic buildings fascinated Larry. He was surprised to find that there weren't many tall buildings. He had expected skycrapers as seen in pictures of New York City and Chicago. Nevertheless, he appreciated the beauty of the ornate and majestic buildings in the center of the city. The trio passed government buildings, museums, churches, and parks filled with memorial statues. They found pubs overflowing with city dwellers and soldiers. And made their way into many of them to raise a pint of their own.

Later in the afternoon, Larry, Vince, and Fred caught a ride on a double-decker bus, raced underneath the city on the tube, and even ventured a ride in a London cab. When they staggered out of the back of the black cab, Vince declared he would rather fly another mission than ride in another London cab![1]

In every pub and store, Larry and his two friends were welcomed with handshakes and words of encouragement. Except for the blackout curtains on every window, bombed portions of the city, and all the military uniforms, the three could almost forget that they were there to fight a war. The holiday revelry in the bars and dance clubs lasted into the night. Eventually, Larry, Vince, and Fred found their way to their room and crashed fully clothed onto their beds.

The next morning, the three headed out to find something to eat. However, on a side street, Vince and Fred found a bicycle shop and went inside to check out the stock. An hour later, they each left with a new bicycle. They hurried to find a restaurant to get a bite to eat before it was time for them to head to the train station and back to base.

After finding a spot on the train to stow their bikes, the guys collapsed into some seats and recalled the highlights of the last two days. They felt like kings while in London, but now they were being morphed back into drones as they returned to the activity of the air base.

In January of 1944, the missions came fast and furious as the American forces were reorganized. The Eighth and the Fifteenth Air Force merged to form the United States Strategic Air Force in Europe under Lieutenant General Carl Spaatz. Lieutenant General James H. Doolittle became commander of the Eighth Air Force based in England and Major General Nathan F. Twining, commander of the Italian-based Fifteenth.

In between missions, Pifer's crewmates entertained themselves by playing pranks on one another and building things to make their surroundings hospitable. In the machine shop, Aiello cut a hundred-pound practice bomb in half to make an ashtray for the barracks. In large letters, he painted the words *Butt Can. Butts Only*, on its side. As a joke, Aiello added another note for Fred Bittner. It read, "If you are colored [*sic*] blind, put your butts in this blue receiver." Fred Bittner may have been color-blind, but he was a good speller. He razzed Aiello about his misspelling for weeks after.

For their accumulating collection of bicycles and parts, the men made a bike rack. During off hours when the weather was nice, they rode their bicycles into the countryside. They became pretty adept as bicycle mechanics and took repair kits with them in case of any unforeseen problems, such as punctures and chain breaks. On one unusually nice day, Pifer, Aiello, and Bittner rode out to see the ruins of an ancient castle some twenty miles away.[2] For the three, as well as for other army personnel at Horham, the bicycle offered an escape from the tedium of military life and the psychological stress of waiting for their next mission.

Early in February, Dunham's crew was grounded temporarily when the pilot had an ear problem. A string of routine missions followed the two-day break and, by the tenth of the month, they had completed their twelfth mission. They were rewarded with a trip to the "rest home." Instead of going to Liverpool where many of the crews went, Pifer and his crewmates headed to Bournemouth on the southern coast of England.

In summers past, the seaside resort had played host to vacationing Brits; now it was a staging area for American army ground personnel. The crew hoped for ten to fifteen days of rest, but instead the Germans bombed Bournemouth every night, keeping them awake and on edge. When someone piped up, "Let's go to London," off they went. Pifer enjoyed leaving the Bournemouth SSO and its classical music behind. The dynamics and crescendo of the classical pieces resembled the noise of battle too much for his comfort, and he had to go outside to get away from it. In London, there were bars with lively "contemporary" music, dancing, and lots of alcohol. The bombing followed them to London, but the men made the best of it and had a good time taking in as much nightlife as they could before heading back to base.

When the crew got back to Horham, a new bomber was assigned to them. They decided to call it *Slightly Dangerous II* in honor of their first aircraft. The bomber didn't arrive in time to allow the crew to paint its nose art before they were sent out on their next mission. This was their thirteenth mission, unlucky thirteen.

In the briefing room on February 25, 1944, conversation ceased when the intelligence officer pulled back the curtain from the map. Colored tape marked the direction the mission would take to their target, Regensburg, Germany, and the Messerschmitt fighter factory that intelligence said was located in the valley there. The Eighth sarcastically referred to the place as "Happy Valley" due to the deadly concentration of anti-aircraft guns.

On all approaches into Germany, German radar stations identified aircraft entering their air space. Hitler's fighter squadrons,

P-51 Mustang. Author's collection.

stationed nearby, signaled when enemy aircraft approached. In an instant, fighters swarmed into battle, directed by the ground radar stations. In addition, the valley was thought to have more than a thousand anti-aircraft cannons. Instinctively, the American bomber pilots knew that more than likely it would be their most difficult mission to date. So when their bombers entered the valley that fateful day, they were not surprised by the ferocity of the battle.

The P-38 Lightnings, P-47 Thunderbolts, and P-51 Mustangs escorted heavy bombers on their missions over Europe. The resilient American fighters intercepted German fighters swooping in and out of battle. Their job was to protect the Allied bombers from attack. The bomber crews admired the "fighting fools" in their fast planes, which zipped in and out and around the lumbering bombers warding them off. However, with the lightning quickness and agility of the fighters came a smaller fuel tank. The fighters' long-distance range was much shorter than the approximately 1800-mile range of the B-17F bomber. Unable to go the full distance to Berlin, the fighting escort turned back, leaving the Fortresses to fight it out alone. It was with regret that the bomber crews watched the fighters turn back toward England.

As the American fighters became a speck in the sky, another band of German fighters zoomed up from the ground. A savage attack began.

In the ball turret, Pifer saw the first of the FW190s at nine o'clock. He reported the enemy fighters' position over the intercom. When their aircraft dipped out of sight, the gunner's intuition kicked in. He felt sure that the fighter planned to come straight up underneath the B-17. The Sturmstaffel 1, a German assault fighter squadron, had a history of ramming bombers.

The Sturmstaffel 1 was an experimental unit formed only in October 1943 and soon to be grounded in May 1944, and merged with an assault group. A military historian would call the Sturmstaffel "radical and fatalistic," as led by Major Hans-Gunther von Kornatzki. When enlisting in the elite German unit, each pilot took an oath to "down a bomber during every engagement or ram it if all else fails."[3]

Before the FW190 could ram *Slightly Dangerous II*, Pifer saw the spat of incoming machine-gun fire and returned it. Shouts came from the bombardier, "Who's firing? That's a P-47!" The ball-turret gunner responded, "If it is, you better damn well tell him to pull away!" But Pifer was sure it was a Focke-Wulf and he was right. Suddenly an Allied bomber came in close and opened fire on the Focke-Wulf and it zipped away. The crew breathed a collective sigh of relief.

The 100th Bombardment Group had come to the aid of Dunham and his crew and they were grateful. Dunham knew that his plane was running low on fuel and evasive maneuvers would surely have used up the last in his tanks. When the bomber landed at its base, it ran out of gas on the runway and had to be towed into the hangar. The quick action of the 100th almost certainly saved the *Slightly Dangerous II* that day.

Missions began to blur into one in February as the Eighth Air Force bombed by day and the British Liberators, joined by the American B-24s, bombed by night. Then the Allied offensive began a push toward Berlin.

On March 3, 1944, heavy clouds blanketed the skies over Europe. For several weeks the Royal Air Force had been bombing Berlin and the American forces sorely wanted to get into the action. The 95th Bombardment attempted and failed to reach Berlin and several aircraft were lost on their return to England. It was the seventeenth mission of Dunham's crew, who were thankful they had returned.

On March 4th, Pifer awakened to another gray-blanketed sky. He joined the rest of the men scurrying from their quarters to the mess hall and various other places on base. Already running late, Pifer shoved his wallet into his pants instead of checking it in and ran toward the briefing room. For breakfast, the cook served fresh eggs. "Not a good sign," he thought. They only got fresh eggs when they were going on a tough mission. As Pifer and his crew members crammed into an already overflowing room, the briefing officer, Major "Jiggs" Donahue, informed them that maximum forces would be dispatched against military objectives in the area of Berlin. "Your bombs must get in there. We've got to smash Berlin, no matter what opposition they put up." Pifer glanced at his crew members. With each mission into Germany they were losing more and more bombers and fighters. Heavy casualties had already been inflicted upon the bomber squadrons that lifted off from the air bases in England. Yesterday's attack had been pure hell, one of the worst they had seen. Pifer prayed they would make it back from this one.

CHAPTER SIX

THE LAST MISSION

For the push on Berlin, the mission commander, Lieutenant Colonel Harry Mumford, assigned Lt. Melvin Dunham as today's flight leader. Thirty-six planes took off from Horham, England, with *Slightly Dangerous II* as deputy lead plane, or second plane, in the group. Green, amber, and red lights blinked in the early dawn of March 4. One after another, the B-17s formed *V*s behind their lead airship. In all, reports claimed approximately five hundred B-17s of the Eighth Air Force took off for Berlin on that "push" day.[1]

Visibility was down to three hundred yards in the predawn light. As they neared Suffolk, England, more identification flares illuminated the sky as more planes took off. The *V*s grew in number. Clouds blanketed the sky over England and did not lift over the North Sea. Inside the flying fortresses, gunners counted off as they test-fired their guns over the water. Almost half-way to the assigned target, about three hundred miles from England, oxygen or engine problems forced some planes to turn back. Everyone and everything needed to be in top form for this mission.

Slightly Dangerous II leveled off at twenty-seven thousand feet over eastern Belgium. Dense clouds, thicker than the thickest fog bank, forced them to climb to twenty-nine thousand feet with the thermometer reading minus sixty-five degrees Fahrenheit.

Shortly after crossing the coast of the continent, the Eighth Air Force ground headquarters sent out a recall signal. As more and more B-17 squadrons turned around, the men on board Dunham's lead airship looked at each other and shrugged. "What is going on?" An uneasy feeling began to grow in the pit of Pifer's stomach. As apprehension mounted inside the remaining flying fortresses, someone in the group eventually broke radio silence and radioed the mission commander. "Sir, the message said we were to return to base."

"Continue to target," Mumford's voice crackled back. "We have not received the authentication."

Every coded signal was followed by authentication signals that verified the integrity of each message, but for some reason no signal followed. The question was whether or not the Germans had introduced the message to steer the bombers off course. Or perhaps they had missed the signal. As planes veered away, heading back to England, Dunham cursed under his breath and continued on toward his target—Robert Bosch AG factory in the Klein Machnow suburb of Berlin.

Lt. Dunham later noted that in the vicinity of Magdeburg, Germany, they experienced heavy flak but did not suffer any apparent damage. However, circumstances changed dramatically at the beginning of the bomb run.

Something was wrong, dreadfully wrong now. Pifer shook his head and tried to figure it out. Then he realized that the number one engine was frozen in the full flat position, causing a heavy drag on the remaining three engines. There was nothing anyone could do and it was too late to turn back. Flak came fast and furious. Suddenly a burst of anti-aircraft fire hit the number one engine and it blew up. From his position in the ball turret,

Pifer saw the propeller blades forced back against the remaining engine. His stomach lurched. "Shit!"

Inside the B-17, the bombardier worked feverishly to drop his payload before the plane crashed. No one would survive the explosion of the B-17 if it crashed with the bombs still in its belly. However, if the bombs were ejected, at least some of the crew had a fighting chance for survival.

Dunham and his copilot, Renner, held a steady course inside the gray cloak of clouds surrounding them. A bomber should never be flying under these conditions, the crew felt. The clouds were as high as thirty thousand feet, well above the normal flying altitude for the B-17. If they could hide their monstrous plane in the cloudbank for a while, there was a good chance that they would be safe from the swarm of German Focke-Wulf fighters that had taken to the air when the attack began on Berlin. "So far so good," thought Dunham.

Lund, the crew's bombardier, yelled that he needed assistance. His remote would not open the bomb-bay doors and he needed help to open them manually. Flight engineer Anderson rushed forward. He and Lund struggled with the crank and finally managed to open the bomb-bay doors.

The bombs fell, giving away their position. The German FW190s swarmed the flying fortress like hungry mosquitoes. Relentlessly, they buzzed around the bomber, attacking it from all directions. The cloud cover lifted, exposing other American bombers. The German fighters no longer had to search for their targets.

Flight Navigator Mathews worked feverishly to calculate their coordinates and relay them to ground command in case the airship went down. Even in the cold interior of the plane, perspiration beaded on the faces of the rear gunners as they swung left and right, firing furiously at the German fighters

Three Sturmstaffel 1 pilots who carried out a relentess attack on the Thirteenth Combat Wing on March 4, 1944, during the first U.S. daylight mission on Berlin. *Top left*: Unteroffizier (Sgt.) Gerhard Vivrous; *top right*: Feldwebel (S/Sgt.) Werner Peinemann; and *left*: Geldwebel Hermann "Dieter" Wahlfeldt. These pilots successfully carried out an attack on the 95th Bombardment Group B-17 named *Slightly Dangerous II*, piloted by Lt. Melvin B. Dunham. T/Sgt. Lawrence I. Pifer was the radio operator and ball-turret gunner. The bomber crashed near Berlin on March 4, 1944. Courtesy of Barry Smith.

darting in and out and around *Slightly Dangerous II*. Thompson, the assistant radio operator, was at his station listening for any high-pitched chatter on the wire, taking messages, and forwarding them to the pilots and crew. The crew had no time to consider their fate.

Dunham hollered, "Pifer, are you in position?" His answer came quickly with a volley of shots from the ball turret at a German fighter just below them. The fighter, smaller and lightning fast in the air, whizzed past and quickly maneuvered to get the B-17 in his sights to fire another barrage of machine-gun fire. The B-17 was struck with a volley of shots.

The bomber descended so rapidly that the glass ball turret froze up like a snowball. Since Pifer couldn't see anything, he backed out of the ball turret and made his way over to Aiello to offer help. Peering out over the waist gunner's shoulder, Pifer could not see any Focke-Wulfs, but he knew they were there somewhere. It was just then that Barstow drew back from his waist guns and stepped between Aiello and Pifer to peer out the right side of the plane.

The crew teased Barstow unmercifully about his curiosity, even nicknaming him "the Curious Cat." He always wanted to know what was going on. During card games in their barracks, Barstow would circle the table of players, peering over their shoulders. Laughing or hemming and hawing at each hand, he taunted the others with his knowledge of their opponents' hands and their lack of it. Some players batted him away in irritation; most just laughed at him.

No one was laughing today. Just when Barstow leaned in, twenty-millimeter cannons carrying double-impact explosives hit the gunners. These shells pass through the first object they hit, usually the outer skin of a plane. Encountering a second object, they explode on impact. The shot sailed through the small waist-gunner's window, passing right through Aiello's body.

Aiello dropped where he stood. Barstow, leaning between Aiello and Pifer, was the second point of contact.

As the shot exploded inside of him, Barstow dropped to the floor of the plane screaming. Clutching his stomach, Barstow cried for help. Instinctively, Pifer knew that Aiello was dead and Barstow near death. Bittner in the tailgunner's position was the only gunner at his station in the back of the plane. Pifer had to gain control of the waist-gunners' machine guns and continue firing or all of the crew would be goners.

In the front of the plane, Dunham lowered the landing gear, signaling to the German pilots to cease firing because the B-17 was going down. The FW-190s did not pull back, but continued their assault on the damaged plane. The command to abandon ship was given.[2]

The copilot, bombardier, and navigator bailed out about eighteen thousand feet from the ground. Anderson, the flight engineer, was still in his position. Suddenly the B-17 came under heavy fire. Anderson returned fire with his guns, as did Pifer in the rear of the plane. When a second engine went out and he lost flight controls, Dunham radioed to Anderson to bail out. "Now!" Dunham heard nothing from the rear of the plane and assumed the others had heard his order to bail out. He did not know that their communication lines had been severed when Aiello had been hit. The pilot moved to the small hatch just ahead of the left side bomb-bay door and jumped.

Inside the tail of the plane, Pifer continued pacing back and forth between the waist guns, firing at the German fighters in hopes of knocking at least one out of the sky. As he moved back and forth, Barstow grabbed at Pifer's pant leg, crying for help. With half of his face blown off and the other half covered in blood, Barstow held on to his stomach, trying to hold in his organs, as he cried out in anguish. Blood soaked the floor of the radio room of the mighty B-17. Freezing out the horror and carnage around him, Pifer kept firing the machine guns.

Bittner moved in from the tailgunner position to check whether Aiello was dead or alive. Silently, he turned and bailed out the rear door of the plummeting B-17. As his parachute billowed, snapped, and swung him gently to the ground, he cried for his lost friend.

Inside the American bomber, Pifer peered out past the gun, fire, and smoke, and realized that during his panic-stricken firing of the machine guns he had missed the "bail out" command. The plane was going down. The tops of trees were looming larger.

CHAPTER SEVEN

THE JUMP

As the plane approached the treetops, Pifer realized he was not going to make it back to England that day. He pulled his chest chute on, snapped it into place, and jumped out the bomb-bay door. Barstow no longer cried out in pain. He and Aiello lay dead.

With relief, Pifer left the grisly and bloody scene inside the plane, and yet he feared what or who awaited him below. As far as he knew, all of his crewmates might be dead. What could he, one man and an American to boot, do behind enemy lines? As Pifer relaxed into a free-fall, he patiently waited until he was clear of the guns of the ball turret and the bomber before pulling the ripcord on his chute. The chute opened with a jolt, yanking him back from the quickly rising ground. A thrill ran through him and he thanked God when he didn't lose his boots—that was a miracle in itself! In training, they were told that often parachuters lost their boots with the jolt of the chute opening. In the bitter cold and snow, Pifer knew he would need his sheepskin boots and heated shoes when he landed.

When Pifer bailed out, he knew the plane was close, too close, to the ground. He feared getting caught in the backwash of the plane when it crashed. Looking up at his chute, he thought it looked awfully small. Did only the pilot chute open? He tugged on the shroud lines, trying to right himself before impact, but it was too late! He crashed to the ground, landing on his left leg and side.

In England, *Slightly Dangerous II*, serial number 42-31785, under the command of First Lt. Melvin Dunham, was reported missing in action after being shot down on March 4, 1944. The report stated that the B-17 crashed at 13:43 hours one kilometer south of the village of Hassel and three kilometers northeast of Stendal after being shot down by two Focke-Wulf 190s. Sixty-nine out of more than five hundred bombers and eleven of the twenty Mustangs that set out that day did not return.

The blow of the impact knocked Pifer unconscious. Coming to, he saw a Focke-Wulf above him and quickly reeled in his parachute to get it out of sight. Pifer was sure the pilot radioed his position to German ground forces. Running, falling, and dragging his injured left leg behind him, Pifer made his way to a cluster of trees growing in the center of a plowed field.

Undercover, the downed airman appreciated the fact that the pilot could have shot him then and there, but did not. Allowing himself a brief rest to catch his breath, Pifer felt his left leg to see if any bones were broken. He was sure his ankle was broken, but so far he felt no pain. Frantically, he buried his chute. Pifer then extricated himself from the bright blue "bunny suit," the one-piece, battery-heated coverall airmen wore in flight. In the distance, the crashed B-17 exploded and flames leapt up from the aircraft. He paused for a moment and watched several people run toward the plane.

At the sight of the German civilians, Pifer fought to regain his composure. He murmured to himself, "Boy—it's a hell of a long way to Spain from here." In the briefing room, the intelligence officer had told them if they crashed to head to safety across the border into Spain. Pifer had an escape map in his wallet that would help guide the way, but for now, he knew he had to put distance between himself and the people at the scene of the downed plane.

The injured airman spied the woods nearby and hurried across the field, over a road, and along a fence row. Farm boy that he was, Pifer tried to make it look as though he was checking the fence, but apparently that didn't fool the crowd surrounding the plane. He heard a shout and looked around to find two civilians, one with a shovel and one with a pitchfork, running straight at him. He pulled out a hunting knife that his father had given him and that he always carried with him into battle, but it was no use. Shouting again, one of the men pointed a pistol at him. Out numbered, the young American threw his knife to the ground and raised his hands in surrender.

Within minutes, German citizens armed with an assortment of miscellaneous farm implements surrounded Pifer. Pushing and shoving him to the ground and picking him up again only to pummel him to the ground again and again, the crowd screamed at him in German. The American airman couldn't understand a word they said. The mob became more agitated and he was sure they would kill him right there. Pifer silently prayed for German soldiers to get to the crashed plane and to him.

Pifer had every reason to be afraid. He knew the first few hours of captivity were often the most dangerous. Airmen frequently encountered hostility when captured behind enemy lines. Citizens were all too anxious to lynch those responsible for bombing their cities and country. Instances of mob attacks rose as Allied bombing increased in the waning years of the war. Prisoners of war (POWs), even when escorted by German guards, were often attacked in villages with stones, clubs, and fists, often fatally.

A few days after Pifer's capture in Germany, photographs of downed airmen being led away by German soldiers appeared in American newspapers. Swedish journalists provided pictures to papers around the world. In the photographs, Nazi guards herded disheveled and obviously injured airmen toward trains and vehicles. Swiss dispatches also reported the lynching of six American airmen captured in Germany. The correspondent alleged that the German command incited its citizens through propaganda fliers. Many who saw the leaflets believed that they encouraged German citizens to kill their enemy if they could and ignore the rules of international warfare.

Although Pifer didn't expect to be lynched, he felt that the stand of trees was too conveniently at hand for the ugly mob. He tried his best to understand what the angry crowd wanted from him. Eventually, through sign language, the American realized that they wanted his parachute and flight wallet.

British and American supply sergeants distributed to each departing airman a wallet containing an escape map, a variety of bills in different European currencies, condensed food or a small block of concentrated chocolate, and items that might assist a crash victim to travel some distance to a safe point. Sealed in tiny bags were Halizone or water purifying tablets and no-sleep pills. A tiny compass, a miniature razor, fishing hooks, and a length of nylon cord rounded out their kit. Each airman kept the wallet in a zippered pocket in the pant leg of his flight coveralls. It was this wallet that the Germans wanted Pifer to surrender.

Hobbling ahead of the mob, Pifer led them back to the tree where he had buried his things. He fell to his knees and quickly dug up the blue suit. A farmer standing near Pifer grabbed it out of his hands. Digging a little farther away from the suit, Pifer uncovered his parachute and gave it to a German girl. European fabrics were scarce during the war and the silk from the parachute could be used to make many things, including dresses. Pifer uncovered the flight wallet and another farmer grabbed it out of his hands.

Pifer did not lead the group to where he had buried his personal wallet containing pictures, addresses, and money, even though it lay in a nearby dunghill. He hoped that someday someone would find the wallet and possibly mail it to his father, but it never did come to light.

Soon, a German soldier appeared waving his gun and pushed his way through the crowd to stand in front of the American airman. He loudly proclaimed in English, "For YOU the war is over!" Stabbing his finger at the prisoner, he began shouting, *"Papier, papier?"*

Puzzled, Pifer looked at him and shook his head. Reaching into his own pocket and producing a wallet, the German soldier waved it in front of his prisoner. Pifer pointed to the German farmer who had taken the wallet earlier. Glaring at the airman, the man reluctantly gave the wallet to the German soldier. The guard pushed Pifer forward and marched him toward a nearby town and detainment. With his head held high, Sgt. Lawrence Pifer, prisoner of war, stumbled forward on his injured ankle. He had no idea where he would end up, but for now he was safe with the German soldier.

CHAPTER EIGHT

CAPTURED

At the edge of the dirt road running along the farm, a German military vehicle waited for the prisoner and his guard. Jamming the butt of the rifle between Pifer's shoulder blades, the guard nudged him aboard the truck with the German soldier at his heels. After a short journey, the truck pulled in front of a jail in a small village, which Pifer later learned was near an air base. When the guard pushed Pifer into a cell, he stumbled and fell to the ground. Before falling, Pifer had seen an American airman slumped against the wall. Now the airman rushed forward and Pifer looked into the surprised face of Bittner, the tailgunner of *Slightly Dangerous II*.

Fred pulled Larry to his feet and asked if he saw any other parachutes when he jumped. As far as they knew, they were the sole survivors of their crew. They then considered the inside of their cell. The six-foot-square brick and concrete room offered no means of escape. They were more concerned at the moment in keeping warm since they had not been given any blankets.

On the bunk, the two Americans sat shoulder-to-shoulder, sharing each other's body warmth. Fred began to tell Larry how he had been captured. A German soldier found Fred in his parachute; he still had on his thermal suit. In the cold, dank cell,

Larry desperately wished he had his suit. Murmuring words of encouragement, they tried to ignore the pain from their injuries.

Bittner had a huge lump, painfully swollen and throbbing, over one eye. It was difficult to determine whether he still had an eye. Larry told him there was no blood, so maybe it was still there. "Did you injure it when you hit the ground?" Shaking his head side to side, Bittner told his buddy that shrapnel ricocheted off the flak suits he had hung inside the tail section of the plane for protection. A piece bounced and hit him in the eye. Larry asked if he could feel any shrapnel in the eye, but Fred said he wasn't sure. He just knew it hurt like bloody hell!

By this time, Larry was struggling with his own pain. The shock from events had worn off and an intense pain coursed through his injured side and leg. He did not know if he was shivering from the shock, cold, or fear. Fred tried to cover Larry with his body and keep him warm so the tremors would stop. Larry mustered all his strength to meet the situation, thankful that a buddy like Fred was with him.

Later in the afternoon, a local policeman brought Pifer his heated suit. Even at ground level and without electricity, the suit was warm and his shivering finally subsided.

Occasionally, the guard would open the door to the prisoners' cell to let the townspeople see the "mighty" fallen American airmen. Each time he did, an old woman would rush in and try to strangle the prisoners with her bare hands. Bittner and Pifer tried to push away the tormented crone without hurting her. The guard leaned on the door frame and laughed. Eventually, a young woman shouldered past him and dragged the crying old lady away. Bittner and Pifer assumed she had lost someone dear in the war. Catching some German words in her raging litany, the two airmen speculated that she couldn't understand why they were alive when her son was dead.

While the prisoners tried to sleep in their cold cell, Walter Cronkite relayed the story of the battle of March 4, 1944, around the world. "American bombers blasted the outlying section of Berlin for the first time in the war today and found the Luftwaffe virtually powerless to meet the historic challenge which opened the daylight offensive against Adolf Hitler's doomed capital." The news reporter claimed that every American airman based in Britain dreamt of annihilating Hitler's stronghold. News accounts of the heroic actions of the American forces, including the new P-51 Mustang fighters, splashed on front pages all over the United States. Mothers, fathers, brothers, sisters, and wives prayed that their daring airmen were safe back at their base.[1]

In all, twenty-one of the 95th and eight of the 100th Bomb Group dropped their payloads over Berlin. The Germans claimed they lost eleven fighters that fateful morning. Reports of American casualties failed to agree. Although it was agreed that the Eighth Air Force lost approximately twenty-four fighters, the numbers of fallen bombers varied. One stated that the 100th Bomb Group lost one fortress, while the 95th Bomb Group lost four. Another claimed fourteen were lost. Military reports in the days following the attack stated that eighty out of six hundred bombers that began the mission were lost. The U.S. Army Air Force and Royal Air Force did not rest, but relentlessly continued the day and night raids over Berlin.

In the early hours of March 5th, a truck pulled up in front of a German jail and a guard roused his sleeping prisoners. Larry's leg was throbbing and he couldn't move. Fred looped Larry's arm around his neck and carefully carried his buddy out of the cell and into the back of the truck. Larry became Fred's eyes, since Fred had difficulty seeing with only his one eye. As they scrambled aboard the waiting truck, Bittner and Pifer were elated to see the other members of the *Slightly Dangerous II* crew.

The two gunners filled their pilot in on their experiences in the back of the B-17 as it plummeted toward the ground and regretfully reported the deaths of Aiello and Barstow. Several of the crew members saw the flames from the crash. They comforted themselves that their fallen comrades were reduced to "ashes" in the fiery B-17 and not left somewhere unburied. In many cases, the Germans left the bodies of dead Allied airmen and soldiers to rot where they fell.

An armed guard sat at the back of the truck near the canvas-covered opening. As a result, the Americans could not see out the back of the truck and had no idea where they were headed. Their conversation lapsed and, trying to ignore the pain in his leg, Pifer distracted himself by making futile plans for what lay ahead. He surmised they were headed to interrogation. In his present state, he hoped he could survive it. One twist of his injured leg and he was sure he would roll over. The fear and tension emanating from his fellow passengers choked the air, making it hard to breathe in the back of the truck as they traveled through the night. Larry glanced around at his crewmates and wondered if torture weighed on their minds, also.

During training in the States and later in England, intelligence officers discussed interrogation at the hands of the. Suggestions were made about what to do in such circumstances, but for the young airmen, some barely out of their teens, facing the reality of interrogation and perhaps torture was overwhelming. The fear of what awaited them was more frightening than death itself.

The truck ground to a halt and the engine turned off. The Americans glanced around at one another. The guard jumped from the back of the truck and shouted and motioned for the prisoners to get off. Emerging from the dark interior of the truck, the prisoners squinted in the early morning light. It was Sunday,

March 5, 1944, a little over twenty-four hours after they took off from their home base in Horham, England.

Outside the men could see that the truck had stopped between some hangars and buildings near a runway. It was obvious that they were at a German airfield. The Americans had no idea where they were, but later learned the base was near Berlin. The bedraggled prisoners marched to a nearby building, where they were introduced to the Luftwaffe command and the interrogation process.

Separating the prisoners one by one, a guard escorted each down a hall and into a room. A Luftwaffe interrogator sat at a table in the middle of a small room. Sunlight came through a single window. Pifer stood glancing around at his surroundings until, in perfect English, the German officer invited him to sit in the chair across from him and have a little chat. Puzzled by the interrogator's American accent, Pifer stood staring at the officer. Again the German invited him to sit, and Pifer did. On the table between them lay two blackened dog tags. One was Barstow's, the other Aiello's.

Stoically, Pifer gave his name, rank, and serial number to every question posed. He thought of his stepmother and how she had beat him. He would not give in now either. His face appeared placid, not showing surprise, fear, anxiety, or anger. He sat with wooden determination. Pifer was able to place a blank mask on his face and hide all his emotions deep inside where no one could ever find them. With surprise, he realized that the years with his stepmother had prepared him for this very situation.

Noting the American's Germanic surname, the interrogator changed tack and chastened Pifer for fighting against his "fatherland." The officer began to recite the history of the 95th Bombardment Group and the 335th Squadron, Pifer's squadron. The German knew where the squadron was stationed in England and was familiar with nearly all of its bombing missions. At the end of the litany, he asked the young American if he had anything to add. Pifer sat quietly, staring straight ahead. A guard entered the room and he was escorted to solitary confinement.

In his cell, the prisoner thought that was a little too easy and wondered what would happen next. A few hours later, guards led First Radio Operator Pifer and Flight Engineer Anderson to a truck. They could see the rest of the crew climb into the back of yet another truck.

When Pifer and Anderson arrived at a railway station and the others did not appear, Anderson said he wondered why the group was separated. They could only speculate that it was because of their injuries since the others were healthy. It was clear that Pifer had a broken leg and Anderson was bleeding from a wound he received during the air battle. The wound was bad and now it bled profusely through his bandages. Larry worried about his buddy, Fred Bittner, and his swollen eye. If indeed they were separated because they were injured, he wondered why Fred had not been sent with him and Anderson.

A short time later, the train came to a stop in Berlin. The guards asked for directions to Hermann Göring Hospital and relief flooded the injured prisoners when they heard the word *hospital*. They indeed were going to get medical attention.

As the small band of guards and prisoners tried to find their way to the hospital, the toll of the crash, injury, and struggle to walk weighed heavy on Pifer. His leg no longer supported him and Anderson tried to help him as best he could. At one point, the hobbling airman blacked out and fell to the ground weak with exhaustion. It was the afternoon of the sixth of March and he had not eaten or drunk anything. His mouth watered at the thought of the chocolate in the escape kit that the German soldier had taken from him. Eventually, one of the guards found a broken tree limb and brought it to Pifer to use as a crutch. Slowly the quartet limped along.

At times the German guards left the injured airmen standing alone on a street corner or in a subway station. Remembering the mobs in the countryside, the Americans tried to blend into the walls of the buildings around them or hide in the corner of a station or cower on the fringe of a crowd to remain unobserved. Their bright blue flight suits made camouflage impossible. The blood from Anderson's injured arm covered both of the prisoners. Most of the people on the street or in the station paid little attention to them, until someone yelled, 'Luftgangsters!' Then a crowd would gather around the prisoners and harangue them. Fortunately, the guards always returned in time to whisk them away before they received any more injuries.

It was obvious that the guards were not from Berlin. Walking up one street and then another, they asked for directions to Hermann Göring Hospital. Several times they got lost. After a number of stops on the subway, the band of travelers reached the station nearest the hospital, even then a long walk lay ahead.

Finally, at the hospital, the prisoners donned institutional pajamas and had their injuries checked. While the two pajama-clad Americans sat in the hall waiting for a doctor, a nurse handed each a cup of ersatz, black coffee cold and bitter. Sputtering and choking after the first swallow, Pifer turned to Anderson and said, "Jesus, what are they trying to do? Poison us?" Anderson roared with laughter. The two were so thirsty, they gulped it down anyway and waited for the doctor.

Eventually, a nurse led Pifer away to a small examining room and a doctor entered the room to set his leg. The doctor explained that there was nothing he could do about Pifer's broken ribs. In another room, a doctor cleaned and stitched Anderson's wound. The flight engineer had taken three hits to his right arm from enemy fire during the bombing run and was now pretty weak from losing so much blood. Orderlies wheeled the two prisoners into a wardroom and the guards who had arrived with Pifer and Anderson took their place outside the door.

The room was on an upper floor of the hospital with a view of the city. However, the patients were too exhausted to observe the panorama and soon fell asleep.

The roar of the air-raid sirens cut through the men's sleep. Startled awake, Pifer didn't realize where he was for a few minutes. From his vantage point, he could see the explosions as bombs hit buildings and houses in Berlin. The explosions lit up the night sky. He looked across at Anderson with a grin and they sent up a cheer. "Go, Liberators!" The airmen were sure the bombers were British because they were the only ones that flew night missions. The American bombers made only daylight runs.

Hospital staff rushed into Pifer and Anderson's room to assist the prisoners out of bed and down the hall. They joined a stream of patients moving to the underground air-raid shelter located in the basement of the hospital.

It was March 7th. For days the flying fortresses of the Eighth Air Force and British Liberators intermittently bombed the German capital day and night. And for hours the weary occupants of the subterraneous tunnels waited for the air raids to stop. When all was quiet, the delayed-action bombs began to erupt and the city became a fiery inferno.

As members of a crew on board a bomber, Anderson and Pifer were used to dropping the fish-shaped bombs and seeing the puffs of the explosions from above. Now the two men experienced what happened when a five hundred- or one thousand-pound explosive hits its target. Despite the pounding and ear-shattering explosions, a tremor of exhilaration ran through Pifer and Anderson. For some twisted reason, they found it satisfying to experience the force of the mighty Eighth's bombs.

When it was quiet again, the hospital staff moved their patients back into the hospital wards. When the bombing runs came closer and closer together, the hospital staff, instead of taking the Americans to the bomb-raid shelter, just locked the door to their wards. Pifer and Anderson sat out the attacks in their room high above the city, exposed, and never knowing if they would survive or die at the hands of their own forces. As buildings exploded around them, they entertained themselves by cheering for the bombers in the sky. The hospital survived to stand for many more days.

The main offensive on Berlin continued until the ninth of March. Bombers returned to drop their payloads over and over again. The hospital began to fill quickly with more downed and injured flyers. As the bombing increased, the frightened citizens of Berlin became frantic. By the twelfth of March, portions of Hermann Göring Hospital lay in rubble.

The German staff and patients in the hospital resented the American and British prisoners of war. On the night of the twelfth, guards sneaked out of the hospital with their prisoners and loaded them onto a waiting train. Not only was the staff fed up with the Allied prisoners, but also the citizens of Berlin threatened revenge on those whose planes had bombed their city and homes.

Meanwhile, at his home in Pennsylvania, Ivan Pifer received notification from the United States War Department that his son was missing in action over Germany since March fourth. His only son was behind enemy lines. On the fifteenth of March, Helen Pifer Snyder received an unopened letter written in February that was stamped "Missing." Her only brother was behind enemy lines.

In Berlin, the train carrying Pifer and Anderson with their guards traveled 336 miles away to Frankfurt. The German guards were taking their injured pajama-clad prisoners to

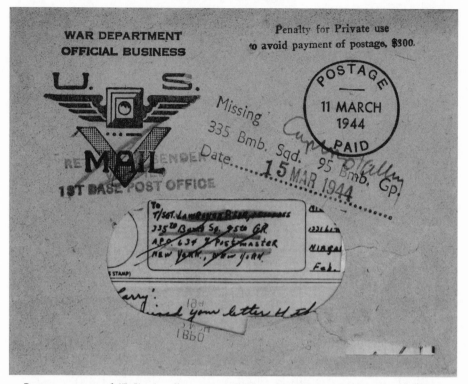

Letter stamped "Missing" return receipt, dated March 15, 1944. Helen Pifer, Lawrence's sister, received this first notification that her brother was missing in action. Courtesy of Lawrence Pifer.

another hospital. Prior to the war, the hospital was a mental facility, but now it served as a hospital and processing center for prisoners of war. Leaving behind the comfort of a hospital ward in Berlin, Pifer and Anderson now entered one of the prison-processing centers in Frankfurt am Main.

Upon arrival, Pifer was asked, and then ordered, by the German staff to sign a stack of papers. When he would not sign the papers, he was placed in solitary confinement. A man introduced as a representative of the Red Cross entered Pifer's tiny concrete cell. "If you sign the papers, you will be released from solitary confinement."

During Pifer's training, American and British instructors had warned the airmen that interrogators disguised as Red Cross members would attempt to get the prisoner's signed confession. Pifer looked at the man standing at the door and his gut told him instinctively not to trust him. He refused again to sign the papers and was left in solitary confinement.

That same day a doctor arrived to remove Pifer's cast and supposedly check his injury. He left the cell and returned to tell the prisoner that there was no plaster to replace his cast, so he would have to lie still in bed until the leg healed.

The only other men seen by Pifer were his guards. Stern-faced guards entered his cell once a day to deliver his meal tray. Other prisoners had their metal trays passed through an opening in the door, but since Pifer was bed-ridden, his tray had to be delivered to his bedside.

Lying perfectly still day after day to protect his ankle, the young man suffered from pain and hunger. Never before had he felt so alone. In solitary confinement, growing weaker, Larry cried for his dead buddies, friends, family, and himself.

A week later, a guard came into his room and ordered him out of bed. He was informed that his recovery period was now over.

CHAPTER NINE

DULAG LUFT FRANKFURT

The guard led Pifer, clad only in his hospital pajamas and slippers, into the street. Two feet of snow blanketed the ground and the sidewalks were slippery as they headed for the trolley station. German command had issued an order that prisoners being escorted through cities, alone or in groups, must use the roadway. In this case, the guard showed mercy on his skimpily clad prisoner and let him use the sidewalk.

Shivering and favoring his leg, Pifer tried to keep from falling on the ice. People gawked at the prisoner as he followed the guard, but did not taunt or harangue him. Once inside a trolley, Pifer soon warmed up.

After a short ride, they arrived at their stop and got off. The two walked toward a brick building that Pifer was sure must be a castle. The ornate building dominated the tropical landscape of the Palm Gardens, the Botanical Gardens of Frankfurt am Main. The Germans had converted the gardens into Dulag Luft Frankfurt am Main, a processing center for POWs.

The German government funneled all prisoners through a Dulag interrogation center or entrance camp (*Durchgangslager*). The word *Dulag* later became synonymous with interrogation.

In late 1943, more than one thousand men passed through the Dulags each month. By 1944, the numbers rose to two thousand and at the peak of the offensive and war in Europe, three thousand men crowded the entrance camps.[1] The transit camps (Dulag Lufts) assigned captured Allied airmen to prisoner-of-war camps (Stalag Lufts) in Germany and its occupied territories. *Luft* came from the German word *Luftwaffe* or Air Force. Infantrymen were processed at a Dulag and sent to Stalags. Civilian internees were processed and imprisoned in Ilag camps. In September of 1943, Dulag Oberursel closed when it was bombed and the German command moved the transit camp to Frankfurt am Main.

Located seven miles northwest of Frankfurt, the camp in the Frankfurt Botanical Gardens sat only 1,635 yards from the main railroad station. Military intelligence reports stated that Swiss Red Cross representatives were concerned that the camp was exposed to attacks from the air, especially since the Allied forces bombed all manufacturing centers, military installations, and major transportation networks that could be used by the Germans to transport military ground troops and supplies. The Dulag Luft was a sitting duck for attack.

In the processing center, a fallen airman or captured soldier officially became a prisoner (Kriegie) of the German Prisoner of War Department. A staff member of the department photographed each prisoner and assigned him a number. Stripped of his identity, personal possessions, and pride, the Kriegie officially became a prisoner of war.

During the processing stage, the authorities accused Pifer of stealing the pajamas to execute an escape. They charged him with stealing property of the German government, which was punishable by court-martial and death. Violations of German laws by prisoners of war, such as willful destruction or theft of

Reich property or disobedience, could be punished under the full extent of the law. German officials even initiated paperwork for Sergeant Pifer's court-martial.

Over and over again, the airman tried to explain to the officials how he had come by the hospital pajamas. Eventually, they dropped the charges. Was it psychological torture, or did they actually believe the young prisoner? Whichever, they issued Pifer a British uniform, coat, and German hobnailed boots. He was given a "capture" parcel containing a safety razor, cake of soap, and a few other toiletries and taken to a five-by-twelve-foot cell. The whistle and clickety-clack of the nearby train bounced off the walls of Pifer's cell. It took a few days to learn to sleep through the noise. He needed his rest to brace himself for more interrogation.

Until the official interrogation began, guards placed their prisoners in solitary confinement. German interrogators typically did not follow a policy of physical violence. They used privation and mental and psychological blackmail to get prisoners to talk. If they did not cooperate, solitary confinement on starvation rations, such as black bread and water, was common, sometimes for days on end. Withholding cigarettes, Red Cross parcels, and toiletries increased pressures upon the prisoners. Interrogators and guards used threats and cursing to harangue them. In some cases, prisoners of war were held in the "cooler" for thirty or more days before being transported to a prisoner-of-war camp. However, most prisoners were moved to permanent camps within three to five days. From long experience, the Germans found that intimidation yielded less return than a more friendly approach.

After three days of stewing alone in his cell, a guard escorted POW 3155, Sergeant Pifer, into interrogation. When Pifer refused to sign a confession apologizing for atrocities against the homeland or to fill out any of the information papers, an Oxford-

educated officer entered the room. He introduced himself as a
Red Cross representative, explaining that it was important that
Pifer give the Red Cross much-needed information about his
crew and their status so that their next of kin could be notified.
The prisoner continued to provide only his name, rank, and serial
number.

While Sgt. Larry Pifer was in the Dulag Luft undergoing interrogation, at home in Clearfield, Pennsylvania, the local newspaper ran an article about him. "Mr. and Mrs. Ivan Pifer received
a telegram from the War Department stating that their son was
wounded and officially listed as a prisoner of war in Germany."
The journalist included the high school that Larry graduated
from, his job history, enlistment dates, and names of family members living in and out of the area.

In Germany, undergoing interrogation, Pifer asked the German officer what he would do if both of his hands were burned
and bandaged and he could not write his signature. The officer
said that *he* would sign for the prisoner. Pifer told the officer that
he would have to do so. Shaking his head, the officer asked if
there was anything he wanted. Pifer thought for a minute and
then asked if he could have one of the cigarettes lying on the
table.

His guards had taunted him by blowing in puffs of smoke
and then closing the door. Inside his cell, Pifer could hear them
laughing on the other side. The officer looked at the prisoner for
a minute, then lit a cigarette and passed it to him. They sat in
companionable silence while Pifer smoked. When the cigarette
was only a stub, the interrogator called in a guard to escort the
prisoner back to solitary confinement.

While Pifer was in solitary confinement, the rest of the pris-
oners entered prison camp life. Beside the main complex of the
Dulag Luft transition camp stood a series of wooden barracks.
In each one, a group of Kriegies was expected to keep the

building and their rooms clean. German command assigned a senior officer from each military force—whether American, British, or French—to be in charge of "his men" and to teach each newly arrived Kriegie the routines and policies of the Dulag Luft. Sometimes that officer was able to tell a new arrival what permanent camp he would eventually be sent to. Even in captivity, the men found something to be happy about—they had an officer of their own in charge and they were with other Americans. As long as they were with their comrades, they felt they could endure anything.

German Command segregated POWs in permanent camps by nationality, rank, and branch of service. During deportation, camp officers were separated from the noncommissioned or enlisted men. In the earlier days of the war, Allied officers had traveled by passenger trains to officers' camps (Oflags) where they were accorded the respect that their position as officers demanded. The Supreme Command of the Wehrmacht directed commandants of Oflags to use only such German guards "as are physically and mentally unobjectionable and who thus are not liable to produce an unfavorable impression on the prisoner of war officers."

It seems that in some Oflags, commandants and others complained that guards were totally unfit for their task because of physical disabilities or low intelligence. The German pride was sensitive to the thought that imprisoned American or British officers would equate their inadequate guards with the entire German Army Services.

However, it didn't matter what the Allied enlisted men thought of their German guards who were lame, deaf, near-sighted, or mentally unstable. After all, the enlisted POWs were only the lower tier of the U.S. Army Air Corp. For the enlisted prisoners of war, guards were guards. There were also separate orders and rules set down by the German Command for the treatment of Soviet, British, and French prisoners. The Soviets were near the very bottom of the prison hierarchy, just above the Jews. POWs were moved to permanent camps—whether Oflags or Stalag Lufts—within a few days after arriving at the Dulag Luft.

POW Pifer left the Dulag on the twenty-second of March. Guards escorted a large contingent of enlisted airmen to the Frankfurt railroad station and loaded them into "40 or 8 box-cars." The term originated during World War I for freight box-cars whose carrying capacity was forty men or eight horses. In this case, six cars were jammed with more than three hundred men, well exceeding the limits of the boxcars. The doors to the freight cars slid closed and a guard wrapped barbed wire around the bolts and the door casters to secure them in place.

Pifer and six other injured prisoners were led to a seventh box-car at the end of the line. Their guards sat beside a warm pot-belly stove at one end of the car, while they huddled at the other end of the straw-lined car. The uninjured prisoners were not so fortunate. It was impossible for them to sit down because of the numbers crammed into each rail car. Instead, they took turns standing and squatting. At least the heat of their bodies kept them warm in the draughty, wooden freight cars. The boxcars were placed in the center of the marshaling yards and left there. As nightfall shrouded the yard, a mournful wailing from the air-raid sirens announced an impending attack. The men in the cars in the railway yard would soon find out that they were the next target of the Royal Air Force.

German anti-aircraft guns began pounding away, launching shells into the night sky. They missed their targets and the British bombers dropped their loads. Bombs exploded, turning the night as bright as day. The guards in Pifer's boxcar scrambled out the door, fastened it shut, and ran away to some nearby buildings. The prisoners could not escape because they were locked inside the boxcars, with no way to get out.

The explosion from the first bomb ignited several nearby rail cars and embers from the small heating stove in Pifer's car spewed onto the wood shavings and straw that covered the floor. The men quickly scrambled to snuff out the flames with their clothes and blankets. They screamed for their guards to come back and let them out, but to no avail. Frightened groups of men clung to each other to wait for the end—to the bombing or to their lives.

For a solid hour the raid continued. Melancholy and despair settled over the POWs as they gave up hope of surviving the bombing. They knew that the tremendous volume of bombs signaled another major offensive by the British forces, and they were in the middle of it. Their thoughts were filled with an intense darkness. One fear replaced another fear until fear was overwhelming. Each passing hour teemed with the promise of death from one source or another.

After what seemed like an eternity to Pifer, the bombs stopped and the guns were silent. Standing by the slats of the cars, the POWs saw flames leaping in and around houses and commercial buildings in neighborhoods surrounding the rail yard. Wild animal-like screams from injured German citizens pierced the night air. Shouts from firemen and rescuers arriving on the scene joined the escalating high pitch of mass agony. People ran out of their houses and apartment buildings to put out the fires.

"Boom, boom!" Delayed-action bombs began to go off one by one. Earth-shaking explosions rocked the boxcars. They sounded like another raid all over again. The prisoners peered through the slats to watch the spectacle. There would be no sleep that night for them or the frenzied Frankfurters who struggled to put out fires and save the injured.

With the first rays of daylight, the German guards returned to the boxcars and opened the doors to let the prisoners relieve themselves. Gasps could be heard up and down the line as the prisoners looked at the incredible sight. Mass destruction everywhere! Fires burned out of control. The railroad tracks looked like huge roller coasters winding and circling in the air over trenches where the bombs had exploded.

Miraculously, the only things intact in the rail yard were the seven boxcars in which the prisoners spent the night. Frankfurt's beautiful glass-domed rail station had been reduced to rubble with wisps of smoke rising out of the heap. Fearful of what the day might bring, the prisoners clamored to be taken back to the Dulag to get something to eat and be near an air-raid shelter. The guards told their prisoners that the Dulag was *"kaputt."* A British bomber had crashed into the camp, destroying it and everything and everyone inside. Shortly after the bomb attack, the Dulag Luft was moved to Wetzlar, fifty-three kilometers from Frankfurt.

As the men gaped at the spectacle around them, they caught sight of a lone building standing amongst the rubble about a half-mile from the train station. "I wonder how the Royal Air Force missed that building," Pifer said. Just then the building exploded before their very eyes.

Huddled into groups, the prisoners watched as the citizens of Frankfurt wandered dazed and confused. About noon, without warning because a bomb had destroyed the air-raid alert system, the Eighth Air Force flew over on a daylight raid—their target was Frankfurt. The guards hustled the prisoners into an air-raid shelter at one end of the marshaling yard.

Crowded together inside the shelter, civilians resented the presence of the Allied prisoners. Arguments broke out between the guards and the civilians. Germans were given precedence inside air-raid shelters, so the prisoners were crammed in wherever they could find room. More and more people pushed inside as the bombing continued. The POWs were allowed to stay.

In order to protect his broken ankle, Pifer went into the latrine, where there was still a little room to move around. He managed to keep his foot elevated by lying on his back on the concrete floor and sticking his feet up in the air. The wall of the small room supported and protected his injured leg from the crushing bodies. Piles of people lay on the floor in any space available. Smoke, rancid sweat, and the rank smell of sewage overwhelmed the crowded space that Pifer lay in, but he ignored it all and went to sleep.

The prisoners and their guards remained hidden in the shelter for two days and three nights, until railroad employees repaired the tracks. Then the uninjured prisoners were ordered to push, lift, and roll the seven boxcars onto them. Engineers and their crews boarded the train and waited for the prisoners and guards to climb into the rail cars once again.

When it came time for the POWs' train to leave, it seemed that the entire populace of Frankfurt appeared on the tracks. Armed with ropes, pitchforks, and other implements, they rushed forward, ready to tear the prisoners to shreds. The German commander ordered his guards to form a ring and cordon off the prisoners. He sent a runner to an army camp for reinforcements to protect the men in his custody. Huddled and chained together, the prisoners nervously watched as the crowd grew angrier and angrier. Some of the Americans felt sure that the civilians would break through the ring and lynch them then and there. Eventually, more German troops arrived and dispersed the angry mob.

As the train moved out of the Frankfurt station, bombs began to explode. Civilians jumped onto the outside of the rail cars, hooking their hands and feet into the slatted walls and climbing to the top or clinging to the sides. As the train rolled forward, more Frankfurters threw their children, family members, and themselves into open cars. Desperation fueled the mass exodus from the flattened city. British bombs had destroyed their homes, businesses, and once beautiful city. Now the Americans were back to bomb what was left. The train offered Frankfurters their only avenue of escape and they didn't even care where they were headed.

Tightly packed into the cars, the men struggled to keep from being trampled by other prisoners and to keep away from the grasping hands clinging to the outside of the car. Angry voices bellowed at the prisoners locked inside their wooden traps. Even though it was extremely cold outside, the men, packed like cattle, were hot. Occasionally, the POWs shifted positions so that others could make their way to the outer edges of the box-cars, where they could gulp in large amounts of fresh air. Arriving in Erfurt, German guards forced the Frankfurt refugees to get off the rail cars.

Once more the train lurched forward and the men in the box-cars stumbled against each other. They passed towns and villages. Peering through the slats, silent prisoners gazed out at row upon row of the black skeletons of bombed buildings. Here and there wisps of smoke snaked up through the wreckage. Bricks and rock tumbled out into the streets. There was devastation everywhere. Silence hung heavy in the air. Even the birds did not sing. It was as though nothing lived. The spectacle was unreal.

Inside the freight cars, the men looked away. It was the bombs they carried in their B-17s, B-24s, and Liberators that wreaked this havoc. The weight of guilt pressed in on Pifer. "Damn Hitler and the Nazis! Damn their war!" he thought.

As the sun sank in the sky, the prisoners realized that the train was heading northeast, but could not even guess where to. American and British air raids frequently interrupted the train's journey. Occasionally, the engineer shunted the train off onto sidings to wait until the bombing ended. Time and again, damaged rail lines forced the train to head in a new direction. Day and night, the train lumbered on through Germany. It passed Warszawa (Warsaw), Poland, and turned north and finally came to a stop.

After five exhausting days on the train, the POWs jumped to the ground in the small village of Heydekrug in eastern Prussia. By this time, the men were anxious to get out of the crowded cars to stretch their cramped limbs, breathe fresh air, and relieve themselves. While en route, the guards allowed the men to take turns urinating just outside the door of the train and then circle back into the cars. Otherwise, the train did not stop unless it was forced to. Now out of the cars in Heydekrug, the Germans lined their prisoners up along the tracks and motioned for them to squat to defecate.

As the men squatted near the tracks, passengers on trains passing through Heydekrug watched, ridiculed, and harangued them. The POWs ignored their hecklers and relished shining their asses at the Germans.

When they turned around, the Americans became conscious of the fact that the Heydekrug station appeared to stand alone, with nothing else in sight. The prisoners, surrounded by armed German guards, began to fear that they had been brought out into the forest of eastern Europe to be executed. But if that was so, why weren't they shot immediately? Pifer's heart raced as his anxiety rose. Damn it, if he could survive the crash, he decided that he could survive whatever lay ahead.

CHAPTER TEN

STALAG LUFT 6

S tanding next to the train that cold winter morning in March of 1944, the prisoners could only guess what was next. Suddenly the guards shouted, "*Raus, raus, raus.*" Already the prisoners were becoming familiar with orders in German and they moved out quickly. The POWs with their guards marched through the snow and mud down a road leading them away from Heydekrug. A short distance from the station a camp appeared. They had arrived at Stalag Luft 6.

When Pifer and the motley crew of airmen marched into camp in March of 1944, they were among the first imprisoned American servicemen in Germany. In June, the Military Intelligence Service of the United States War Department reported that 24,367 American men were prisoners of war in European nations. By the end of the war, the number of prisoners in Europe would rise dramatically to 92,965, according to a November 1945 intelligence report.

Located near the old Prussian-Lithuanian border, Stalag Luft 6 was approximately forty kilometers northwest of the town of Tilsit. The Stalag accommodated three compounds for enlisted men: one American, one British, and another with a mixture of

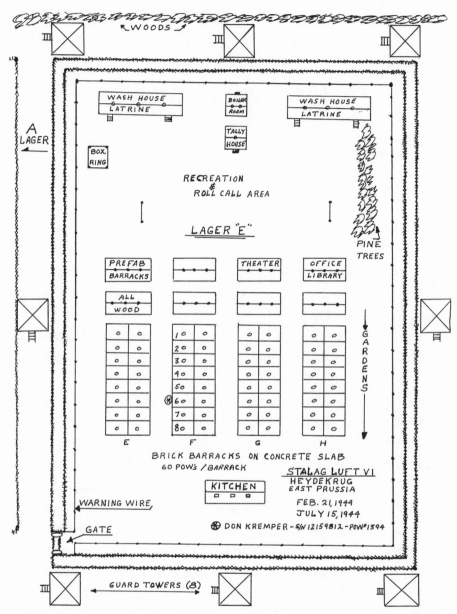

Sketch of Stalag Luft 6, Heydekrug, E. Prussia, drawn by ex-prisoner of war no. 1394, Donald Kremper, who was imprisoned in Stalag Luft 6 from February 21, 1944, until July 15, 1944. Courtesy of Donald Kremper.

British and Americans. The prisoners entered the outer ring of the camp, which was the German administration and guard compound (*Vorlager*). Glancing around, Pifer saw German officers and guards walking between buildings and other guards with machine guns in towers off to his left and right. There was no time to linger. The guards kept a steady pace and moved the prisoners into the inner compound.

The men entered the sole gate into the American compound and passed through a series of barricades that included a double row of wire fences six to eight feet high, with guard towers strategically placed around the perimeter. Just inside the gate, a two-foot warning fence of barbed wire surrounded the inner sanctum of the compound and parade ground.

Tired, hungry, and frightened, Pifer was filled with despair as they entered the permanent camp. The despair soon turned to elation when he spotted some fellows that he knew! As the new internees marched into camp, a large crowd of POWs had gathered to see who they were. Pifer spied Hilliard Parish, a fellow radio operator who had trained at Walla Walla, waving at him. Tears sprang to his eyes as he smiled back at Parish. Pifer figured that he didn't face an immediate death sentence because his buddy was still alive.

As the men turned to follow the fence line to the other end of the yard, they passed a wooden building that they learned later was the kitchen. Not one of the new arrivals said a word while passing four brick and concrete barracks. Men gathered near the perimeter fences in the British compound, watching. Americans walked the yard or stood in small groups talking until they saw the new prisoners marching in. Conversation ceased and they searched each face for a familiar one in the line of newcomers. March, march, march. It would become a familiar refrain. At the end of the barracks, the compound opened onto a muddy, frozen expanse.

Small wooden buildings were lined up east to west along the parade grounds. At the ends of the grounds, soccer goal posts stood like sentinels unsuited to their surroundings. There were four brick barracks and ten wooden buildings in the compound. Two of the buildings were washhouses and latrines. A small wooden shed or tally house stood between the latrines facing the parade ground. Three of the prefabricated buildings, Pifer later realized, contained a theater, office and library, and overflow space. The camp spokesman (*Vertrauensmann*) for the Allies, T/Sgt. Frank Paules, and a small group of men met the new prisoners at the parade ground in the recreation area to welcome them. The sergeant knew the men were overwhelmed with fatigue, hunger, and emotion at the moment and he kept his introduction short.

Paules and the barracks' leaders decided where to place the new men. There were nine units in each barracks, identified by a letter painted near the door. Each unit or room housed sixty POWs. The leader of Lager E assigned Pifer to Room 6 of Barracks F. Pifer followed the barrack's leader to his room.

The German command allowed the prisoners to pick their own leaders and the prisoners were well organized. All the leaders in Lager E were American enlisted airmen. Gerald Benzel of Navarre, Ohio, welcomed Pifer to the group. As room coordinator, Benzel reported to a barracks coordinator, who in turn reported to the camp spokesman for Lager E, Paules. Each spokesman was responsible for "his" Lager and its day-to-day coordination. After the newcomers were rested, Paules explained the rules and regulations of Stalag Luft 6 to them. It was also his duty to assist prisoners in obtaining clothing and parcel allowances, as well as getting any necessary medical attention, which Pifer certainly needed. A secretary, Joseph Harrison, and a translator, Bill Krebs, helped Paules in these functions. Paules appointed his secretary and translator, but allowed his men to pick their barracks and room leaders.

The commandant of the Stalag Luft 6 was Oberst Hoermann Von Hoerbach. All Lager leaders reported to the commandant. The men considered Commandant Von Hoerbach a fair and just man. Rumor had it he had been in an American POW camp and was repatriated to Germany. His fair treatment in American POW camps influenced his leadership at Stalag Luft 6. Unfortunately, not all the men under Hoerbach's command were as generous as he was.

In Barracks F, Benzel added Pifer's name to the bottom of the roster for Room 6. He introduced the new arrival to the men who packed the room. They were everywhere—standing around, sitting at the table, and lying in their bunks. It was overwhelming to Pifer. There were too many names to remember, but he would have plenty of time to learn them later.

On the walls of Room F-6, double bunk racks ran the length of the long, rectangular room. Five slats, strategically placed, supported the mattress and head, shoulders, back, rear, and feet of its occupant. Each prisoner stuffed a sack with wood shavings and leaves for his bed. Waiting for Pifer was a mattress on a lower berth, which would be easier for the injured prisoner to get in and out of.

Men who had been in camp for a while, had lockers or boxes to store personal items. A few had little more than the clothes on their back when they arrived, but others had layers of clothes and makeshift packs. If utensils were available, each new arrival was issued a spoon and knife to put in his locker or box. Benzel gave Pifer a set and warned him not to lose it. If he did, he would have to make a new set from tin cans.

Many prisoners fashioned cups and containers from the tins in their Red Cross parcels and bartered with others to get table

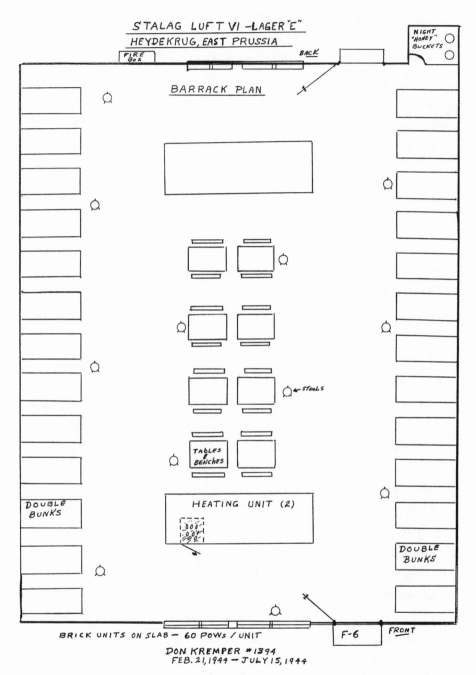

Sketch of the plan of Room 6, Barrack F, Lager E at Stalag Luft 6.
Drawn by Donald Kremper. Courtesy of Donald Kremper.

knives from guards. Pifer became very popular with the men when they found out he had a can opener. He was the only one in the room who had one. He quickly realized that the only way he was going to hang on to his precious utensil was to appoint himself the one and only "can opener." From that moment on, the opener went no further than his army dog-tag chain and his hand.

Two wooden tables with benches sat in the center of the room. A small heating stove, for coal or wood fires, slightly warmed the room and was used for cooking as well. When guards closed the shutters of the windows at night, the room quickly filled with smoke from the stove. So the men fashioned a chimneystack from discarded tin cans. After days without food and sleep, the new arrivals in Room 6 wanted only to find something to eat and a place to sleep. Pifer would have to wait until the next day to get medical care for his throbbing leg.

A hospital for the critically injured or ill was located in the Vorlager, but POWs did not want to go into the Vorlager since so many who did were never seen again. The others were never sure if the patients died of their injuries or were transported out of camp. So the prisoners of Lager E set up an informal first-aid room in one end of a barracks. Near a cabinet in the small barren room was a table and two chairs for the "doctor" and his patient. Two cots stood in the corner by the stove. A steady supply of coke made it the warmest spot in the compound, but medical supplies were scarce or nonexistent. Heat alone could not cure the ailing prisoners.

Medical personnel persistently begged for the desperately needed medications and surgical equipment. Red Cross officials heard their pleas for medicine during their quarterly visits and sent in supplies, but if there was a shortage in the German sector, medicine did not always reach the inmates' infirmary. Prisoners who had some medical experience staffed the first-aid room, but most were not trained physicians. An English medical officer and doctor, Captain Pollack, also a prisoner of war, was allowed to rotate through the three compounds to attend to more serious cases. All medical personnel were volunteers and received no compensation for their work or time in the clinic.

A medic apologized for not having any plaster to set Pifer's leg, but was able to splint it for him. He recommended that the injured airman stay off the foot to allow it to heal and told him to begin to exercise slowly after three to four weeks. A room-mate helped Pifer back to their barracks, where he collapsed on his bed. Pifer's ankle was swollen and painful after walking and marching on it during his transfer from the Dulag Luft to Stalag Luft 6. He was exhausted from the pain in his leg and fell asleep quickly.

• • •

The ultimate fate of each prisoner depended upon his treatment in prisoner-of-war camps. After World War I, on July 27, 1929, forty-seven nations signed a formal "codification" of international law at the Geneva Convention in Geneva, Switzerland. The treaty prescribed the handling of prisoners of war by a detaining power. Both the United States and Germany had signed. Japan and Russia did not. Because they did not sign the treaty, neither country was legally bound to its provisions. That proved to have devastating consequences for prisoners of World War II in the Pacific Theater. Prisoners of the Japanese government suffered excruciating treatment in their prison camps, where slave labor was often the norm. As reports leaked out of the South Pacific Theater, horror-struck American commanders in the States were powerless and could do nothing for their captured male and female prisoners. The forty-seven nations that did sign the treaty found it was to their advantage to observe the international laws to assure reciprocal treatment for their troops.

In 1864, the Red Cross was founded at an international convention in Geneva. It was an organization that would impact the lives of many young men and women during World War II. The Red Cross registered prisoners, inspected prison camps, processed and delivered mail and parcels, and more importantly, supplied food to POWs. Countries such as Great Britain, Argentina, Canada, and the United States packaged literally thousands of tons of goods to be sent overseas to prisoners of war.

A typical Red Cross parcel was ten inches square and four and one-half inches deep. German postal customs allowed only packages weighing eleven pounds, and they were adjusted accordingly before shipping. Contents varied but generally consisted of dried fruits, canned meat and fish, crackers, cheese, tinned margarine, dried milk, jams, chocolate, instant coffee, cigarettes, and soap. Pifer likened the chocolate, or "D-bar," to a slab of baking chocolate divided into three sections about one-half to one inch thick. The "Klim" can, or powdered milk can, in the Red Cross package became nearly every prisoner's bowl.

The food packages were shipped to Lisbon, Portugal, where trucks met the shipment and drove them on to Geneva, Switzerland, to be warehoused until the German command allowed distribution. The intent of the Red Cross officials was for packages to be delivered once a week to prison camps. One parcel was designed to feed one man per week. German commandants were to ensure that each prisoner received a box. However, with Allied forces bombing roads, bridges, and rails, shipments arrived sporadically. Sometimes weeks passed before a shipment arrived in the POW camps. Even then, many commandants did not immediately distribute packages, but instead warehoused the shipments in the Vorlager just outside the reach of the men who desperately needed the rations.

German guards inspected the coveted packages upon delivery. Each can was punctured with a bayonet to keep prisoners from stashing food supplies for an escape attempt. Occasionally, a prisoner would get lucky enough to receive a can that was not punctured and would quickly sew it into his clothing to save for another day. Leaving it in a locker encouraged theft. Starving fellow prisoners or guards during inspection periods confiscated any loose cans. Pifer learned quickly to stash unopened cans and packaged goods in the inside lining of his coat and in his pant legs.

When parcels arrived in camp, the Germans reduced meals until they felt the food parcels were gone or American command complained the men were starving. Prisoners became creative in stretching their packages. Many an hour during a day was filled creating new recipes from the contents of Red Cross parcels. POWs shared their recipes or combined ingredients to make a meal. Chunks of corned beef or Spam were added to soups or mashed potatoes. Men shared cheese and crackers. Margarine, in tins packaged by Cudahy of St. Louis, had an awful metallic taste, but the men used it to hide the sawdust flavor of the bread. They cooked meals in their barracks, or were served by the communal mess hall. A runner reported to the mess hall at assigned meal times to collect the room's food in a bucket. In the barracks, he distributed the meal to his comrades.

Prisoners of war soon learned that the quality of meals would vary with supplies the camp kitchen received. As the Allied forces bombed Germany, they interrupted German shipments of food and supplies. If there were only enough edible foods for the German guards, the prisoners had even less appetizing fare at mealtime. When food was in short supply, confiscated Red Cross packages supplemented meals in the communal prison mess hall. Many POWs were lucky if they got seven hundred calories per day. Officers in prison camps fared better than the enlisted men.

In Stalag Luft 1, officers received twelve hundred to eighteen hundred calories a day, until the fall of 1944. As the number of prisoners skyrocketed, even the officers were lucky to get eight hundred per day. A typical daily allotment could include six potatoes, one-fifth loaf of bread with margarine and marmalade, a small piece of meat (usually horse meat), two vegetables (beet, cabbage, turnip, parsnip, or kohlrabi), barley soup, and tea and coffee with sugar. On the other hand, an enlisted man at Stalag Luft 6 received three potatoes, a cup of soup, one-seventh loaf of bread and margarine, and a half-cup of ersatz coffee made from ground barley or dried acorns. Meat might be served on a weekly basis. When potato rations were low, turnips and kohlrabi replaced them. Meals often featured soups of the day, a concoction of unseasoned water, potatoes, confiscated Spam, and cabbage. Three days a week, German bread wagons circulated through camp distributing black bread to the barracks. The black bread was made of rye grain, sliced sugar beets, "tree flour" or sawdust, and minced leaves and straw. As supplies diminished, the indigestible sawdust became more and more the main ingredient.

To wash down their bread, prisoners made a weak coffee. In order to stretch his ration of instant coffee granules, Pifer wet his spoon with saliva or water, dipped it into the granules, and let it dry. When Pifer wanted a cup of coffee, he boiled some water, then dipped his coffee spoon into his cup just enough to color the water, saving the rest for later. After the "coffee" spoon dried again, it was stored away for his next cup.

With their stomachs partially filled, keeping warm in the frigid temperatures inside the barracks became more important.

In Pifer's Lager, the prisoners got one coal a day for their stove. It barely kept them warm or cooked their homemade meals. They had to decide whether to keep warm or cook. Many times Pifer and his buddy just added layers to keep warm. They put on all their clothes, snuggled close together on the bunk, and threw a blanket around themselves.

Each prisoner's wardrobe consisted of wool and cotton pants, wool and cotton shorts, wool and cotton undershorts, and heavy and light undershirts. If he was lucky, a Kriegie had two pairs of socks, a scarf, a sweater, handkerchiefs, and a belt. Standard-issue blouses or shirts, a jacket, light overcoat, and woolen over-coat rounded out his wardrobe. If they were available that is. Although the list may seem pretty extensive, prisoners generally did not receive new clothes but, rather, castoffs and worn-out items. Each man hoped for two outfits (winter and summer). As items wore out, they were repaired over and over until there was little to discard. They were not often replaced.

Each room leader kept a logbook and a list of each man's name, size, and needs. When Red Cross parcels of clothes or German castoffs arrived in camp to be distributed, the room coordinator referred to his list and attempted to get needed items for his men. Toiletry items, such as towels and shaving brush, were included on the list. If a prisoner was lucky, his two outfits would last the entire time he was in a POW camp, which could be as long as a few months to a few years.

Pifer was lucky enough to get a British overcoat. The long wool coat fell to his calves and provided much-needed warmth in the unusually frigid temperatures of the winter of 1944. He soon traded cigarettes for a knitted cap from a fellow prisoner. The POW with his southern drawl was popular because of his knitting capabilities. He got yarn from Red Cross deliveries or from recycling old sweaters and knitted hats with earflaps for fellow prisoners for a small charge. This ingenious knitter found himself not wanting for food or toiletries. He was able to get more food and clothes than others in camp who were less skill-ful. Sliding the warm hat over his ears, Pifer felt he got a good trade for his cigarettes.

CHAPTER ELEVEN

A KRIEGIE'S DAY

As though it wasn't bad enough to be confined to a prisoner-of-war camp, locked doors barred Pifer and the others from leaving their room. Stalag Luft 6 guards removed the blackout shutters from the barrack windows at exactly 8:00 A.M. and closed them between three and four in the afternoon during the winter months and at eight in the evening during the summer. A guard switched the lights to the barracks on in the morning and off at night. Guards controlled every aspect of their lives and Pifer, like many of his buddies, railed at the very idea of it.

The role of the German guard was to keep his prisoners off balance by replacing respect with fear. By letting the prisoners think they would be beaten or placed in the "cooler" for infractions, the guards were able to control the large group of airmen. Every so often a prisoner would be beaten for no apparent reason other than being in the wrong place at the wrong time. The tower guards occasionally sprayed bullets across the compound to keep the men from gathering into groups and planning escapes. Well-trained German shepherds patrolled the perimeter of the camp, accompanied guards into compounds, and participated in searches for escape tunnels. Often the dogs were allowed to attack prisoners.

During the evening lock-up period, internees were not allowed to walk about the compound area. One morning a mess hall worker inadvertently passed too early through a barracks door that had not been locked the night before, and he was shot on the spot. When the prisoners heard the shots, they ran to the windows. German guards gathered around the man and carried him away on a stretcher. The rest of the prisoners were held in their barracks until later that day. They learned from Paules that the man died in a German hospital in Heydekrug. Staff Sergeant Walter Nies's death and burial were recorded in the *Barbed Wire News*. The uncertain terrors of prison life kept the prisoners in line.

The breakfast whistle came shortly after the barracks doors were unlocked. Instead of eggs, toast, bacon, and coffee, Pifer ate a wedge of black bread and a strong, bitter cup of ersatz. Imagining breakfasts at home or in the army mess hall helped make the dry bread bearable, but later his stomach cried out for more. After breakfast, another siren blew.

It was time to line up for roll call (*Appell*). "Straight lines, men!" The lines stretched around three sides of the parade ground. In front of the tally house, a small group of German sergeants waited. One strode to each end of the line and began to count. They reported their numbers to the guard sitting in the tally house. Somewhere along the line the two sergeants would lose count and it was back to the beginning. Over and over they counted the group until they were satisfied all were present and accounted for. A bunkmate leaned over and told Pifer that for grins some of the guys squatted on one count and stood up to be counted on the second count. "It drives the goons [German noncommissioned officers] crazy," he whispered.

Roll Call (Appell) at Stalag Luft 4. The Germans called roll call twice a day or more if they chose to have a barracks check. A German guard at the camp took this photograph and the rest of the photographs at Stalag Luft 4. The guard traded the photographs for contraband. Sgt. Frank Paules, camp spokesman, carried the photographs back to the United States after liberation. Courtesy of Donald Kremper.

Roll calls took place twice a day, morning and night. If guards suspected an escape attempt, they called roll during the day and checked dog tags against a prison roster. In order to cover for a missing prisoner, a Kriegie or POW lined up and was counted with his dog tag, then ducked and moved down the line to wear the missing airman's tags. This game could and did go on for days at a time until an extremely sick prisoner was able to return to the line or enough time had passed to let the escapee put distance between himself and the camp. Illness did not excuse anyone from roll call. If the barracks were searched during roll call, shouting guards dragged ill prisoners out to the lines. Frustrated and furious tally counters often forced prisoners to stand in line for hours, even in extreme cold or heat.

After dismissal, prisoners wandered away to their respective barracks or to the washhouse. Others reported to work crews. Pifer's injured ankle kept him from finding any real employment in camp, so he returned to his bunk to elevate his foot and rest. When Pifer learned there were farm work crews, he decided to sign up for one after his ankle healed. Other camp work assignments included cleanup, latrine, or burial duty.

The care of the bathhouses and latrines employed several prisoners. A chief engineer and his assistants worked on latrine duty from 6 A.M. until darkness. The twin buildings were 26-by-130 feet and divided into four sections. The main privy hall in each building consisted of two rows of twenty-six covered holes.

Urinals fashioned out of a sloping, tarpaper-lined trough ran down the center of the building. According to an article titled "Super Duper" in the *Barbed Wire News*, a newspaper published by and for American prisoners in Stalag Luft 6, the slope served two purposes: gravity flow and allowance for short or tall prisoners. The chief engineer bragged that it could "easily accommodate fifty customers at once in rush hours." With anywhere from three to four thousand men in a compound and with dysentery rampant in camp, it was always rush hour in the latrines.

In spite of every effort to keep clean in camp, Pifer awoke one morning with a dreadfully itchy scalp. A nearby bunkmate confirmed that he indeed had lice. Lice and skin diseases plagued almost every man. When the lice were especially bad, delousing days began. All the men in the infected barracks took a soapy three-minute shower with a medicated soap. In the kitchens, a work crew took the infected clothes and steamed them in ovens to kill the lice. The crew brought the clothes back to the Kriegies and returned to their kitchen to cook the day's meals.

A wall separated the "sinks" from the latrine. Men lined up in front of two long wooden sinks or troughs that filled the center of the room. With torn scraps of towels or cloth for washrags and, if lucky, a Red Cross bar of soap, they leaned in under the wooden water pipes hanging at shoulder height to capture some of the trickling water on their heads and upper torsos. The troughs caught the run-off and it flowed into the drain that led to a storage tub. Each bather learned to be quick or lose his chance at the water basin. Pifer became adept at lathering and washing quickly.

Overcrowding at Stalag Luft 6 allowed showers only once a week or every two weeks, and then the opportunity to shower was rotated among the four barracks or however many barracks were in a given compound. Fifty-five men shared eleven showers per shift, and shifts ran throughout the day. A partition separated the main water tank from the showers, but otherwise there was no privacy when showering. Four hand pumps manned by rotating groups of prisoners supplied the pressure to force the water from the tank to the showers. A veritable traffic jam of men rotated in and out of the lavatory.

The last room in the bathhouse was the clothes washhouse. Work crews heated water in four kettles on built-in stoves. They poured the hot water into the tubs and long sinks, where lines of prisoners washed their clothes and once a month their bed sheets, if lucky enough to own sheets. As the war went on and the number of prisoners increased, sheets were no longer washed. That simply wasted water. A large dilapidated washtub caught the overflow water from the showers. With soapy clothes in hand, men lined up to rinse them in the tub. The last guy who got to the tub rinsed his clothes in water as dirty as his clothes had been in the first place.

Because it was difficult to keep the waste system flushed, sanitary conditions were deplorable. The latrine crew dumped waste-water into the latrines to carry the sewage away from camp. If there wasn't enough water pressure to push sewage out through the pipes, a sea of mud surrounded the washhouse. The stench in the summer was overwhelming. Clouds of flies rose and fell as men passed through the swamp on their way to the latrine. Buzzing mosquitoes spread disease throughout camp.

Another work crew performed camp funerals. When a prisoner died from natural causes or was killed by guards, a crew of American POWs hauled the body beyond the perimeter of the camp to a communal burial ground. The crew dug the hole for internment and performed a brief ceremony. Compound leader Paules recorded the deceased's name and removed it from the roll call list. The crew left one dog tag on the body to identify the remains. The German command collected the second tag to pass it along proper channels so that next of kin could be notified. It was a grim detail; for some men even boredom was better than facing this material reminder of daily death.

Other crews worked in nearby villages, clearing debris after British and American bombing raids destroyed the buildings. Trucks carried them into a village and guards watched as prisoners filled in holes left by the bombs or pulled down buildings that threatened the safety of the townspeople. At times, guards loaded prisoners onto trains to take them into the cities to clear debris or tear down buildings. However, most crews stayed in close proximity to the prison camp.

During the growing season, some prisoners plowed, planted, and harvested crops on farms near the camp. The airmen preferred farm details because they were able to pilfer food from vegetable gardens. When his leg was healed, Pifer asked for a farm detail and was denied. Even explaining that he was a farm boy did not persuade the German sergeant to change his mind.

For the prisoners who were lucky enough to be on a work detail, even burial detail, time passed quickly. For the others, the days dragged on. The war behind the barbed wire was filled with disease, hunger, brutality, despair, and boredom. There were no training sessions. No bike rides in the country with a buddy. No missions to fly. For the majority of the men in Stalag Luft 6, days stretched out long and empty. Overcoming boredom often meant survival.

Pifer wanted his leg to heal properly, but he was going crazy lying in his bunk day after day. He couldn't help but wonder how long he would be in a prisoner-of-war camp. There were no Allies on the ground on the continent. Germans were every-where and the Stalag was way up north. "God, I might be here for the rest of my life!" He tried to focus his thoughts elsewhere and found it easier to fall asleep to forget.

He always awakened back in the barracks, where he had too much time to think about his situation. He was always hungry, and food rations were meager. There was only so much to talk about with his roommates. After rolling out of his bunk, he would often hobble to the end of the table to see if he could join a game of cards.

The American YMCA supplied the prisoners with sports equipment, games, and cards. Pifer learned how to play a mean game of chess with his compatriots. Bridge games and poker games turned into tournament sessions, especially during the winter months.

As time passed and warm spring days stretched into sum-mer, Pifer began walking and exercising his ankle. He wanted to be physically prepared for the unexpected. He knew that the Germans moved large groups of prisoners to other camps when overcrowding became a problem. Drawing in deep breaths of fresh pine-scented air and feeling the sun on his back raised his spirits. He watched as others played flag football or volleyball in the recreation area of the parade ground.

Pifer loved to play volleyball and one day when he thought his leg felt exceptionally well he joined a game. The ball sailed high in the air, headed right to Pifer. He jumped, being confident he could smash it over the net. Three pairs of arms tangled and the men crashed to the ground in a heap. A roar went up as the ball cleared the net and the team won. Pifer lay sprawled on the ground. He was the only one who heard the snap of a bone in his ankle. He groaned as he thought about another five weeks of recuperation.

Lloyd Holtberg and Leslie Tedman hauled Pifer up from the ground and carried him to the infirmary to get a set of crutches. The American medic said he couldn't wrap the injured man's foot because there wasn't any tape. Spying a set of crutches in the corner, Tedman asked for them. When the medic said no, the frustrated Tedman replied, "Yes, we are gonna take them! I don't see anyone here big enough to stop me!" Looking up at the large man in front of him, the medic shook his head but didn't move to stop Tedman, who handed the crutches to Pifer. Pifer hobbled on his crutches back to the barracks.

A destructive range of emotions wreaked havoc on men in captivity. German guards completely controlled the actions of each POW. No man was allowed to think or act for himself. Being confined to small spaces with thousands of men and little opportunity for privacy made men irritable. Anger festered and eventually fights broke out. Eruptions ended instantly with the pugilists hugging and nursing each other's physical and emotional wounds. A good deal of the time, prisoners struggled to support and prop up each other's emotional morale with words of encouragement. They weren't always successful.

Homesickness preyed on the minds of the men in Stalag Luft 6. Pifer wondered what his buddies were doing in the States and wished he had stayed in Walla Walla with Danny. When Dan heard that his friend Larry had been listed missing in action, he sent Larry's Christmas letter to his dad and asked him to keep it safe. Dan feared that eventually he might have to deliver Larry's last letter to his grieving father.

The futility of their situation in camp often overcame the most stoic of men. As days became months, even years for some, men lost faith that the U.S. Army would win their release from the German prisoner-of-war camps. Fiercely, each airman tried to retain his self-identity through prayer or mental exercises, but for some the stress became too much. It was easy, all too easy, to lose faith in God and themselves. Sadly, some men became "wire-happy"—a term the men coined for a POW who had succumbed and mentally lost control. The wire-happy often committed suicide as a means of escape.

One day, in a moment of solitary bliss, Pifer lay against the sun-baked boards of his barrack. It was as though time had stopped and he was blessed with his fondest wish to be alone for five minutes. As a boy, his favorite times on the farm came when he was alone with the cows in the barn or working in the fields. He prayed for solitude in camp, but it was impossible due to the sheer numbers of prisoners. "How did I get lucky enough to find a place without anyone else around?" he thought to himself. A shadow darted by.

Covering his eyes from the glare of the sun, Pifer watched a lone figure dash for the warning fence, hurdle it, and clutch the chain fence. One shot burrowed into flesh and the man fell to the ground. Prisoners ran toward the downed airman, but guards ordered them to stop. The wire-happy prisoner lay dead on the ground. Larry sat in the sun with his back against the building, stunned by what he had just seen.

Other prisoners would not wait for their comrades to free them from prison. They set to work planning an escape. Escapes were more common and for some reason more successful in the British prisoner-of-war camps. The POWs that were most successful at eluding recapture were those who spoke German and disguised themselves to look like German military personnel. Many of the American military personnel imprisoned in Germany were first- or second-generation European immigrants to the United States. Some of the flyers spoke German as well as their grandparents and parents. Although his grandparents spoke German, Pifer had learned only two to three German words as a child, and they were greetings. Now he regretted that he had not learned more from his grandmother and grandfather. He could have been one of the bilingual airmen.

Behind the blackout shutters, prisoners altered military clothes with dyes, patches, and buttons to resemble German military uniforms. Craftsman melted lead gathered from cans and foil to fashion intricate German, Austrian, and Czechoslovakian medals. Navigators and map enthusiasts plotted the hills, towns, and routes of the region onto paper and cloth, if they did not have an escape map. When completed, the maps were sewn into the lining of coats, britches, and shirts. Money smuggled into camp or bartered for on the POW black market was hidden with maps. Men hoarded food rations. A confidence man assisted the prisoners with their break-out plans, but remained in camp to coordinate a cover-up.

German "ferrets" or special guards, who concentrated on anti-escape measures, were always on the lookout for escapees. Even though the prisoners became adept at covering up for their escaped buddies, guards with German shepherds were soon on the trail of the escaped prisoners.

While in Stalag Luft 6, Pifer watched and assisted a group of men who worked on a tunnel under their barracks. Guard dog patrols circled the camp and its buildings during the night. The keen ears of the dogs discouraged the prisoners from digging then. When daylight came, they moved the stove, under which they had chiseled twelve inches of concrete, lifted the floorboards they had laid down to support the stove, and lowered themselves one by one into the tunnel to dig with cans used for that purpose. A chain of men in the tunnel fed the dirt back into the barrack.

Pifer could not dig with his injured ankle, but he lined up in the barrack to fill his pockets with dirt and hobbled out the door. His overcoat hung nearly to the ground and had a wonderful supply of pockets. Cautiously, he watched the guards pass on patrol and waited until it was clear for him to scatter the dirt around. He had to be careful that the guards would not notice any freshly fanned dirt trails on any muddy spots.

If the guards noticed any new dirt, the ferrets were called in. When "Crowbar Pete" appeared, the prisoners hollered a warning, "Goon's Up!" Pete would plunge his metal bar into the ground looking for a tunnel. If the men in the barrack were lucky, and they were, the bar did not plunge into the tunnel, but they feared detection enough to stop digging until the Germans relaxed their vigil.

One particularly rainy and muddy period in March, an unlucky German guard stood too long over an unshored portion of the tunnel. He sank to his knees in the flooded tunnel. The furious and red-faced guard, mired in the mud, screamed. All hell broke loose. Sirens blew. Guards from the Vorlager rushed in. Prisoners ran to report to roll call before they were shot dead for lingering. The muddied sergeant stood in front of the compound prisoners until all were counted and recounted to verify that no one was missing. An evil smile crossed his face. The punishment for that incident was standing at attention on the parade ground for three straight days in the rain. A crew of prisoners filled in the tunnel and joined the line when they were done.

In April, a group of officers from the German Schutzstaffel, an elite guard of the National Socialist Party, came to visit Stalag Luft 6. The camp guards ordered the prisoners to fall out. A murmur ran through the line as a small group of black-uniformed men strode to the front. "SS Officers. What the hell are they doing here?" someone whispered.

The German Prisoner of War Department was divided into two divisions: the Wehrmacht and the Luftwaffe. The German Wehrmacht, or Armed Forces, generally oversaw prisoner-of-war camps for ground forces captured in Germany and its occupied territories. The Luftwaffe oversaw the camps for air force personnel. Thus, the appearance of the SS was extraordinary. A shudder of fear ran through the young men standing before the group of black uniforms.

With grim faces, the American camp leader, Paules, and his assistants stood at the front of the line of prisoners. One of the SS officers stepped forward and announced that fifty officers from Stalag Luft 3 were dead. They had faced the firing squad after attempting to dig an escape tunnel. Anyone found participating in such an action would face the same fate. All tunneling at Stalag Luft 6 stopped. During his internment at Stalag Luft 6, Pifer reported that there were no successful escapes, but tunnels were not the only means of breaking out.

Frequently men on work crews tried to escape. One particularly ingenious escape attempt took place in Compound E— ingenious up to a point. Two men in Compound E decided that a crew removing Red Cross crates was their avenue out of camp. A six-man detail left the compound with a cart piled high with boxes. One, two, three, four, five, and six. The guard counted the departing prisoners in the detail. Six men must return to the inner sanctum of the compound. What the German did not realize was that one man lay underneath the pile of boxes. Appearing as natural as possible, the six prisoners unloaded the boxes by a building in the Vorlager. Carefully, the crew kept themselves and the boxes between the German guards and the escapee. They built a fort of boxes around their buddy and headed back into the compound with their cart. One, two, three, four, five, and six. The satisfied guard turned away.

The next day the box cart made a second trip into the Vorlager. Another man entered the "fort" of boxes. Now there were two. Six men went out and six men came back. The guard turned back to his watch. The men behind the barricade of boxes waited for nightfall.

A cloudy mantle cloaked the stars and moon, providing cover for the escapees. Only now they had to sneak by the guards' barracks and the staff buildings. A searchlight swung round and round. Peering from inside the fort, the airmen counted the seconds between the arcs of light. First one crawled to the cover of a darkened building. Then the other slithered across the ground. Seconds went by before they dared move toward the barbed wire fences that lay between them and the flat area near the front of the camp.

The screech of a siren pierced the air when the arc of a light bounced past, then back to the second airman. Guards and dogs ran into the yard. Shots rang out. The two escapees dropped to the ground. Dogs leapt on the two men, tearing away at their clothes and at their arms shielding their heads and faces. Someone pulled the dogs off. The second escapee stood up with his hands in the air and immediately fell as shots passed right through his body. His motionless body pinned the first airman to the ground. Guards pulled aside the body of T/Sgt. George Walker and hauled S/Sgt. Ed Jurist away to solitary confinement.

On May Day 1944, six comrades buried Walker with military honors under a clear, blue sky near a stand of young birches. Camp spokesman Paules turned in Walker's dog tag to the German commandant. In solitary confinement, Jurist heard taps playing for his escape partner. He mouthed a silent prayer. The commandant ordered an investigation into the incidence, but nothing came of it in the end. Although there were many attempts to break out of German prisoner-of-war camps, no one was ever sure of the exact number of men who successfully escaped from them.

Spring came with drier weather and hints of green in the woods. For many of the POWs, bouts of depression lifted as the sun rose higher and higher in the sky. Longer days provided more opportunities to exercise and expend energy outdoors. Roads previously mired in mud dried out and Red Cross trucks delivered rations to the camp.

Many of the British airmen had been in camps for years and learned that combating boredom with exercise and the arts enhanced survival. When the Americans increased in number, they followed suit in their own compounds.

Barracks and compound leaders coordinated football, boxing, and baseball games. The American YMCA supplied sports equipment for POWs. The *Barbed Wire News* reported that "promoter" George Pratt of Boston was organizing a two-day International Boxing Show. The German command was persuaded to allow intercompound participation. Pugilists from the Army Air Force and Royal Air Force would participate, but British audiences had to stay in their own compound and watch through the fence.

In preparation for the show, the boxers trained and sparred with each other. In his own training program, Pifer jogged and did calisthenics to strengthen his healing ankle. Promoter Pratt spent a great deal of time circulating through the camp building, touting the mighty muscles of his fighters. He claimed five thousand spectators were expected, so smart ones would get to the matches early! Finally, the day arrived.

Shortly after noon, Pifer and his bunkmates made their way to the makeshift boxing ring. AAF spectators were on one side and RAF on the other. Like a carnival barker, the announcer drew in the spectators, promising the greatest sports spectacle ever staged! One prisoner reported the announcer's words: Lumberjacks from the Northwoods, Steel men from Pittsburgh . . . Rail workers from the Pacific coast . . . Texas cowhands carrying the Blue of the Pratt Stable will compete with RAF and RCAF boxers from Britain, Scotland, Wales, Australia, New Zealand, and South Africa!"[1] The POW said the barker was even more entertaining than the bouts.

For two days, the boxers bounced, circled, and pounded their opponents. The spectators howled at each other across the wire. Men made bets using cigarettes. Rows of German guards supposed to be overseeing the prisoners enjoyed the bouts as much as the prisoners. The final climax was a bout between the AAF and RAF favorites. When the RAF's fighter went down for the final count, shouts of joy and huzzahs erupted in the American compound.

Not all activities were sports-related. Some prisoner-of-war camps created theater groups that put on plays and comedy shows in the evenings. Creative stagehands and crew designers fashioned sets from Red Cross crates and junk. With the friendlier guards, prisoners traded cigarettes for clothes to make into costumes. The Kriegie newspaper proudly announced that the theater group had created a "flashy show house" and it was the "Show Spot of the Baltic." The house held only two hundred men besides the actors, so shows ran for several nights. Talented artists from within their own ranks instructed and directed the would-be actors. An internee, Tom Edwards, who was a Boston vaudeville man prior to his draft, developed and choreographed many of the camp shows.

The camp's library was a coveted commodity. Prisoners donated books that their families sent from home. Red Cross shipments of books arrived when the German command allowed them. The American compound claimed that its library had a collection of six thousand books and a librarian. The librarian and his staff, all prisoners, checked out books and organized educational courses taught by other prisoners. Subjects ranged from banking to foreign languages. Many young men came home after the war and headed to college, attributing their desire for more education to the time they spent in camp classes.

One resourceful POW and former journalist founded his own newspaper. He boasted that the paper, *Barbed Wire News: The Krieges Only Kolumns*, had the largest number of readers per copy of any newspaper in the world! T/Sgt. T. J. McHale, editor and publisher, explained that the reason was simple. German regulations, censorship, and a shortage of printing materials allowed only one copy of each issue.

When his copy was finished, McHale posted the latest issue on the camp bulletin board. Crowds surrounded the board near the recreation area and muscled their way to the front to read it or hollered for the closest man to read it aloud. When the prison camp broke up, McHale smuggled thirty issues of his newspaper out of camp by sewing them into the lining of his coat.

After the last chow call for the day, Pifer and the rest of the prisoners fell into formation for the evening roll call. They had a few more hours to enjoy before the whistle blew for them to head to their barracks. Failure to hit the latrines one last time would mean using the portable pot or "honey bucket" that night. Some nights, a "reader" visited each barracks before lockdown and spread the latest news gathered from the nightly BBC report picked up on the camp's secret receiver.

The reader was an airman who literally read notes taken from a BBC news report. He traveled from barrack to barrack, read the report, and destroyed the note. Each day a different reader would appear so that the German guards would not notice a pattern. The camp radio receiver was assembled daily when radio operators appeared to supply the part they kept in secret. The parts were traded for on the black market or smuggled into camp. Radio transmissions supplied a surprising amount of information on military movements in Europe, as well as world news.

At the camp's assigned time for lockup, guards fastened blackout boards into place. The doors closed and locks clicked shut. Small groups formed to play cards. Others climbed into their bunks to read or write in their logbooks until the lights were switched off for the night.

CHAPTER TWELVE

HEYDEKRUG TO KIEFHEIDE

The men of Lager E awoke July 12, 1944, to the sounds of shouts and running feet. The noise jolted Pifer awake. He realized with a start that the "fall-out" order that he had expected had arrived. Orders were given to get gear together and report to the recreation yard.

The men of Room 6 shoved all their belongings and any loose canned goods into knapsacks they had made or gotten on the prison black market. Some had cardboard suitcases that the Red Cross issued prisoners. Men crawled under their beds to retrieve personal items. Others brought cans, books, and journals from hiding spots and quickly shoved them into their pockets and bags. Since he did not have a bag, Pifer put on all the clothes that he had and shoved his toiletries and silverware inside his coat pocket. Elbows banged heads and men tripped over each other while getting ready. The noises out in the yard only heightened the tension in the room. However, there was no time to contemplate what the fall-out meant.

A month earlier, over the camp radio receiver, the prisoners in Stalag Luft 6 learned that Allied Forces had stormed the beaches of Normandy on the morning of June 6th. Spirits rose in Compound E when the airmen heard their forces were now on the continent. The POWs were sure that ground forces would soon be there to save them. Pifer knew he would never forget June 6th. That day he received two—TWO—bowls of barley soup! He still couldn't figure out why the Germans gave them extra rations that day. After all, it wasn't a victory for the Germans.

More recently, rumors had spread through camp that a German radio news bulletin reported Stalin's Red Army had stepped up its drive into eastern Prussia. The operators of the prison communication system went into overdrive listening to the BBC reports as often as possible, even risking detection by the German guards. Operations' receivers picked up that the Russians had actually gained control of the southern rail lines and were pushing north into East Prussia. Incoming prisoners confirmed the rumors. The POWs hoped the Russians, who were closer than their American buddies, would reach Stalag Luft 6 on the Baltic Sea before it was abandoned.

In preparation for a "fall-out" or liberation, the Kriegies had worked at sewing cans of food into their clothes or hiding them in their knapsacks. Their hopes of being set free were dashed with the orders to fall out. The sudden forced march could only mean that they were being moved ahead of the Red Army's advance.

Pifer's heart raced as he was shoved into a unit and assigned a combine buddy, Wayne Moeller, a bunkmate. He looked at Moeller and wondered if the fear he saw in the man's eyes was a reflection of his own. As the July sun beat down, the navy wool coat he wore hung hot and heavy on his shoulders. Moeller had his coat on as well, and sweat rolled down his face. However, they could not afford to leave their coats behind; they might need them later. A guard came up and shoved a Red Cross parcel into their hands. Pifer and Moeller did not have a bag to carry their food parcels, so they shoved the precious boxes into their coat pockets.

The other prisoners in Stalag Luft 6 watched as the men of Compound E marched with their heads held high in parade formation. The band of airmen passed through the gate and joined a group of British prisoners on the main road out of camp. Groups of two to three hundred men were formed and assigned guards. Pifer and Moeller twitched nervously as they waited for more men to arrive in formation. Eventually, the order to move out was given. *"Raus, raus!"* "Move, move!"

As Pifer and Moeller kept step with the group, Pifer could not help but wonder if they were headed to their own execution. He had heard through the rumor mill that prisoners often were marched out to mass gravesites and shot to death. Fact or fiction, he pushed the thought from his mind. He reminded himself that he was a sergeant in the Army Air Corps and concentrated on keeping in step with the others.

Between July 12 and 14, waves of men departed Stalag Luft 6. Eleven hundred Americans and nine hundred British prisoners marched out of camp on the twelfth of July. Over the next few days, more prisoners left Stalag Luft 6 for camps deep inside the boundaries of Germany. The last prisoners of Compound E left on Friday, July 14, to join the advance groups.

The dust rose up around the feet of the chained airmen as they marched down the dirt road toward Heydekrug. Ripened stalks of grain swayed in the breeze that passed over the fields.

Pifer thought of his father bailing hay. The green fields dotted with grazing cattle and horses formed a counterpoint to the golden hayfields. Farmers hoeing in their vegetable gardens glanced up as the men marched past. Women hanging clothes on lines near their houses turned to stare. The woods on the other side of the road tempted many a man to make a dash, but the chains held them back.

It was only a two-mile march to the railroad spur at Heydekrug. The prisoners regretted that their time outside the wire fences and prison compounds was so short-lived. They marched to the rail cars heading west on the tracks. Once the chains were removed, the prisoners clambered aboard the cars. There weren't enough cars, so more than fifty men crammed into each one.

It took half a day for the slow-moving train to reach the port city of Memel on the Lithuanian coast of the Baltic Sea. The rail cars pulled onto a siding. German guards jumped off the train and stood in small groups, smoking and laughing. Someone walked over and pointed to a Russian barge docked a short distance away. The guards threw down their cigarettes and moved toward the rail cars.

The Germans had seized the *Masuren*, a Russian coal barge, early in the conflict. A hammer and sickle scarred the side of the ship. Booms made out of wire stuck out from the side of the barge, presumably to catch mines planted in the Baltic Sea. A minesweeper anchored nearby would lead the barge as it made its way to the port of Swinemünde.

When the doors opened, the prisoners were told to get off the train. The men jumped down from the rail cars, across the pier, and onto the barge. Guards at the end of the gangway took the bags and suitcases from those prisoners who had them and threw them into the hold in one large heap. Another directed the prisoners to climb single file down the ladder into the bowels of the barge.

As more and more men entered the hold, the group pressed farther and farther into the dark underbelly of the barge. The heat became stifling. The darkness of the far corners terrified some of the men. Their eyes clung to the single shaft of light from the opening above, as they pushed through the others towards it. A small group of prisoners near the pile of bags attempted to sort and return them to their owners. Pifer was glad that he had all his belongings on him. He was sure that many of the guys would never see their stuff again. It was just too hard to identify the bags.

The engines of the barge roared to life and inside the sound was almost deafening. Some British airmen sitting near Pifer and Moeller yelled that the Baltic Sea was so heavily mined that almost certainly the barge would hit a miscreant bomb, or night bombing raids would surely blow the barge out of the water. British bombers routinely dropped mines into the Baltic Sea to interrupt shipping. Even if the barge was not hit during the night, the ship's bow had only to brush one of the mines to detonate it. Occasionally, a bang against the hull or a loud scraping noise caught everyone's attention. More than once, Pifer thought, "This is it! We are goners." The only thing left to do was hope and pray that the minesweeper didn't miss anything and that it would safely lead the barge across the sea.

Several times a day, a large bucket passed through the doorway into the hold below. It swung back and forth until it was lowered enough that someone was able to grab it. The "honey bucket" had arrived.

Passing the bucket, or climbing over men lying three deep to get to the bucket, POWs relieved themselves. When the bucket was full, they hollered for a guard to pull it up. Occasionally, the bucket would tip and the men below would get a shower of urine and feces. Most of the airmen tried to wait, hoping that they would get a chance to go topside to relieve themselves. As the temperatures rose inside the barge, the stench of sweat, vomit, and feces was unbearable. Pifer allowed himself to lean back against the men around him and willed himself to sleep.

In the morning, the door opened and the prisoners climbed out of the hold toward the fresh air and lined up to relieve themselves. Suddenly a commotion broke out at the rear of the barge.

Everyone scrambled to look over the side of the ship. A man was in the water swimming towards shore. Someone yelled, "He's *krank*! He's *krank*!"

Ignoring the pleas that the man had lost his senses, the guards swung their machine guns towards him. The prisoner flailing in the water became still.

The rest of the prisoners stood silently watching the current buffet the body before it sank as the barge steamed forward. The man's combine buddy explained, "The guy said he just couldn't let his mother see him the way he was. He was sure he was losing his mind and could not face another day of prison, crowds, marching." He paused and gulped, "I didn't realize that he meant to kill himself."

It took the barge about three and a half days to reach the port city of Swinemünde, Germany, on the Pomeranian Gulf. Many ships lined the docks and it was quite awhile before the prisoners were unloaded.

After more than three days on the barge, the airmen felt wobbly on their legs and swore they could still feel the rocking motion of the boat. Now they knew why they flew and did not choose to sail. Moeller bumped against Pifer and laughed. As they set out, the men weren't sure whether they were marching in a straight line. Pifer said, "Hell, what does it matter anyway!"

They marched to a second set of rail cars near the docks. The sick were lifted into the first car and the rest climbed into cars behind it. As the POWs waited for the train to leave, they could hear voices, trains coming and going, and the noise of the city. For some, the sounds reminded them of home, and tears blinded the eyes of several men.

Hours passed. A day came and went and still the train did not move. Around midday, another barge arrived at the port and more men from Stalag Luft 6 disembarked. They were herded into rail cars that had been pulled up and connected

to the train. New guards arrived to relieve those from Stalag
Luft 6.

Stalag Luft 4 guards shackled the prisoners' hands and then
their feet to their combine partners. Once everyone was back
on board the train, and as the sun sank in the evening sky, the
train lurched forward and headed south.

After the extremely crowded conditions on the barge, the
crammed boxcars, even with their wooden slats, offered not
much relief in the hot, humid July sun. In Pifer's rail car, the
men, most of them wearing overcoats and knapsacks, were
crowded into one end. Guards sat at the other end. As the temperature rose, sweat poured off the men. Pifer removed his
coat, but the heat, exhaustion, and lack of food made him feel
dizzy and he was afraid he was going to be sick. He couldn't
even get away from Moeller's body heat, because they were
shackled together.

As the ranking man in his rail car, Pifer took command and
described his plan for sleeping. In unison, they would all lie
down. In unison and at his command, they would all shift left
or right in order to roll over. Closing his eyes, Pifer tried to sleep.
But lying so close together, it was bloody hot. As bodies cramped
and someone begged to turn over, Pifer hollered out "roll" and
they all moved in one motion.

The rhythm of the train on the track allowed the prisoners
only fitful resting periods. The sun rose, beamed mercilessly,
and was just beginning to sink when the train slowly stopped
in front of a small station in a heavily wooded area.

CHAPTER THIRTEEN

THE GAUNTLET

Through the slats of the rail car, Pifer read *Kiefheide* on a sign on the side of the station building. The station was the only building visible. No village was in sight, but it was actually hidden in a dense pine forest that the prisoners later learned ran between Stargard and Belgard. The town was on a spur line off the route between Memel and Tilset. Guards pulled open the doors to the rail cars and began to yell, "*Raus, Raus!*"

Blinded by the sun and weak from hunger and exhaustion, the prisoners stumbled and fell as they jumped from the cars. Once on the ground, prisoners helped the sick and injured from their rail car. It was a relief to get out of the cars for a while. Everyone stood expectantly, waiting for the next command.

A red-haired Nazi officer, Captain (*Hauptmann*) Walther Pickhardt, spoke and some young sailors herded the prisoners together into lines, removing the long chain that connected the units of men. The combined partners still remained chained. Shouting at the prisoners and inciting his men, the captain made it clear that this part of the trip was meant to be hell. Navy, army, and Luftwaffe guards, even police dog units, surrounded the prisoners. A few SS men in their black shirts stood at the front of them. Orders were given. Guards fixed bayonets on the ends of their rifles.

About a hundred yards from the station, a ruckus broke out. The red-haired captain shouted, *"Macht schnell!"* "Hurry up!" Chained together, the prisoners found it difficult to get any momentum going. Some of them intentionally dragged their feet, refusing to be ordered about. His face turning a bright red, the captain screamed and struck out at his own men to get things moving. The dogs leapt at the prisoners, and bayonets began jabbing at the men on the edge of the group. Guards cursed and spit at the prisoners. When an airman stumbled, the butt of a rifle crashed into his back.

Relief guards lined the road. A guard breathing heavily from the run fell out and a replacement fell in line. Along the road, Pifer spied machine-gun nests. As he ran, dodging bayonets and sidestepping snapping and snarling guard dogs, he began to worry that they would all be mowed down by machine-gun fire. He wasn't going to slow down to find out and kept running with Moeller beside him.

Madness enveloped them. Prisoners on the outside were jabbed with bayonets and hit with rifle butts. Weak from heat exhaustion, some stumbled and fell. Guards ran into the melee to jab the fallen with their bayonets, often stabbing repeatedly, trying to get the prisoner to stand up and run again. Bloody bodies lay on the road. Snapping and snarling dogs chewed on the easy prey who were lying face-down in the dirt. Friends tried to help those who began to lag from exhaustion, but in the end self-preservation overruled their actions. Pifer and Moeller tried not to step on their prostrate buddies. "Keep going! Keep going!" they urged each other.

The sight of bloody bayoneted men kept them running for their lives. How long would they have to run? Some tried to shed their coats, packages, and bags in order to keep up. With

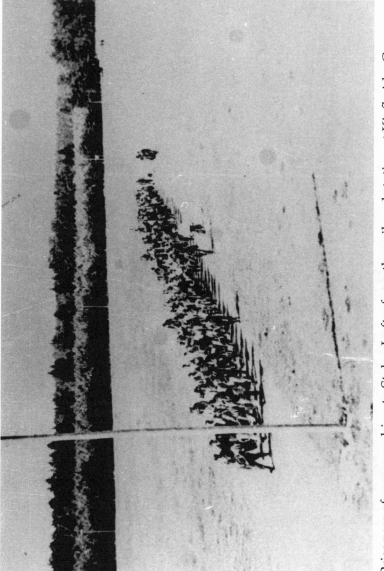

Prisoners of war marching to Stalag Luft 4 from the railroad station at Kiefheide, Germany. Date unknown. Courtesy of Donald Kremper.

The German administrative area or Vorlager of Stalag Luft 4, viewed from a guard tower, 1944. The low brick building in the center of the photograph is solitary confinement where prisoners were placed for committing infractions of the rules. The other buildings are barracks for German camp guards. The guard tower in back is at the southwest corner of Lager A. Courtesy of Donald Kremper.

Prisoners of war entering Vorlager at Stalag Luft 4. The buildings they are passing are German guards' barracks. Guards used German shepherds to patrol the camp and to keep prisoners in line when they marched to and from camps. The horse and wagon to the left of the line of prisoners is a latrine wagon. Courtesy of Donald Kremper.

survival uncertain, it was better to drop their parcels and keep running. Books, Red Cross packages, and knapsacks lay in the dirt.

Pifer began to think that an instant death might be a blessing. Struggling to breathe, he ran and ran and ran. As the frenzied prisoners rushed forward, they tried to stay clear of the guards' bayonets and avoid the packages and clothes that littered their path. More and more men had to carry their combine buddies as they ran and stumbled down the road. Moeller kept pace with Pifer, and Pifer was relieved. He could hardly keep himself going, let alone drag Moeller too. "Is that a clearing ahead?" he panted. "Please, let it be a camp, please. Yes, it is!"

The evergreen trees opened onto a clearing and a partially completed prison camp lay before them. A wall of wire fences separated the line of men from the camp. In strategically placed positions, towers offered guards a clear view of the entire camp, including the perimeter of the Stalag Luft.

A hush hung over the prisoners as they filed into the Vorlager. Men collapsed and lay, not even caring if they died.

Guards separated casualties from the main group. Some bloodied men were so weak, their combine buddies had to carry them to an infirmary inside the Vorlager. Others, with less severe injuries, were treated by fellow prisoners. No one was ever able to gather an accurate count of those who died on the run from the station into the camp, or even of those who died in the infirmary as a result of their injuries.

One man who carried his buddy into the infirmary came out with tears streaming down his face and a bloodied shirt in his hand. His buddy gave him the undershirt, saying his friend would need it more than he would where he was going. It was torn sixty-four times where bayonets had pierced it. The distressed man swore that, if ever liberated, he would carry the shirt home with him to show authorities. Anger and a deep sullen hatred for the guards rose up in the hearts of the captive airmen.

CHAPTER FOURTEEN

STALAG LUFT 4

G roups of men lay on the ground or stood around dazed and bewildered. They did not know what was expected of them. No orders were given. They just languished in no man's land and waited and waited.

Then a small group of Germans carrying bundles came around the corner of one of the buildings and walked toward the tired, ragtag group of American airmen. When the Germans drew nearer, they threw down their bundles in front of the prisoners. Someone directed bands of men to set up the tents. Pifer and others scrambled forward to help. As dusk enveloped the camp, the men finished pitching the tents.

No one brought the famished and thirsty men food or water. Little groups of men pooled their Red Cross parcels and ate what food they had left after the bayonet run. Many food packages had been wrenched from the hands of prisoners and more than half of them had no rations at all. Eventually, guards allowed the POWs to go to a nearby pump to get water.

As the last of the men got water, the guards ordered them into the tents. When no more men could crowd into the small tents, the rest fell asleep on the ground around and between the tents and within the wider circle of guards. In the damp chill of the night, Pifer and Moeller pulled their coats around their bodies and tried to sleep on the hard ground. They did not get a tent, but thankfully it did not rain. They would stay two days in the Vorlager before moving into the main camp.

In the morning, a whistle blew. "Line up!" A small, bulky man in his mid-thirties strode out of a nearby building. He barked an order at a guard near him and the prisoners were ordered to remove their clothes. A small group of sneering guards moved in to strip-search the new arrivals. A guard unit rifled through the prisoners' pile of clothes, pulling out trousers and coats. Protesting prisoners were silenced when guards moved toward them with guns drawn. A tall thin guard with glasses and a mean-faced giant of a man shoved the prisoners into line. The latter said, "They are going to men who need them more than you do!" When their belongings and remaining clothes were returned, the men entered Stalag Luft 4.

Stalag Luft 4 was located near Hammerstein, Pomerania, approximately one hundred miles northeast of Berlin. The camp had opened in May of 1944 and construction was not completed when the men arrived in mid-July. The clearing around the camp, hidden in a heavy pine fores, was about one and a half square miles.

Although Compounds A and B were completed, German nationals and prisoners were still working on Compounds C and D. Small tents stood in a row near some barracks, housing the overflow in each compound. Twenty-six men piled up like matchsticks into seven-man tents.

Sgt. Richard Chapman of the Army Air Corps greeted the newly arrived prisoners and asked, "Who is in charge?" Men at the front of the group told him that the Germans had taken their camp leader and interpreter away. Gestapo security guards had singled out Frank Paules and his assistant, Bill Krebs, as they entered the Vorlager and led them off.

Photograph of Lager A after it was completed in 1944. Note the low warning wire fence extending approximately fifty feet in from the main fences. The mound with three vents between the barracks is the potato cellar. The small building beyond it is the counting house. Lager B can be seen beyond A. It was under construction at time of the photograph. To the right of the row of guard towers, other compounds are being constructed. Courtesy of Donald Kremper.

Lager A barracks 1, 2, and 3. The rolled tents stacked on the ground between barracks were used for prisoners who found no room in the barracks. Courtesy of Donald Kremper.

Sgt. Chapman told the new prisoners that most of the men in Stalag Luft 4 had been incarcerated for only a few months. He went on to explain that the commandant, Aribert Bombach, recognized himself and Victor Clark, a Brit, as camp leaders for the prisoners, but that did not mean that they had much voice over the conditions in the camp. He cautioned them that Captain Walther Pickhardt was in charge of the guards in camp and a man to be wary of. "Stay out of his way!"

Chapman suggested they find a place in the tents near the barracks and set up the tents that they had been given earlier beside the others. All the buildings were filled to capacity. Prison crews and German nationals were working on two new compounds and, hopefully, they could soon move into them. He explained that food and supplies were desperately needed, but pleas to the commandant fell on deaf ears. Food shortages would continue into the fall.

In September, a Red Cross shipment came into camp, but even then conditions did not improve. At the end of the month, prisoners stood near the warning fence and watched as a truck left camp with their shipment of clothes. They suspected that food had also left the camp. The commandant would not let the American and British camp leaders verify shipments with the invoice, so they never were sure if they got an entire shipment or a portion of one. Through October, the prisoners received half-rations and most of the time the kitchen served them sauerkraut and brown bread.

Shortly after the prisoners from Stalag Luft 6 settled into Compound A in July 1944, Paules and Krebs, haggard and bruised, entered. The commandant made it clear to Paules that he would not be camp spokesman at Stalag Luft 4. Only one leader was needed and Chapman would be it. Commandant Bombach wanted to drive a wedge between the prisoners' loyalties and keep them in constant turmoil so that he would be in complete control of the situation. However, the loyalties of the men from Stalag 6 lay strongly with Paules. To emphasize his supreme command, Bombach appeared to encourage guards to beat Paules and Krebs for the slightest infraction. Paules, instead of breaking, became even more determined to protect and lead the men who had given him their respect and alliance. Be damned if the German Gestapo and SS would run *this* camp.

During his incarceration in the Vorlager, Paules learned the true story behind the bayonet run and what the administration of this Stalag Luft had in store for its prisoners. The SS soldiers laughed and told him that the bayonet run was staged to get prisoners to make a dash for the woods. Hidden machine-gun nests filled with guards waited to mow down escapees. The Nazis wanted a reason to shoot to kill and were disappointed when they did not get to fire their guns.

Inside his cell, Paules seethed when he learned that the camp doctor, Oberfeldwebel Fahrnert, diagnosed over two hundred dog bite and bayonet wounds as sunstroke casualties. After days of torment, he and Krebs were finally escorted into Compound A to join their men. Chapman greeted Paules and welcomed the chance to hand over command to the more experienced Paules, but Bombach never did officially recognize Paules's role in camp.[1]

Red Cross representatives toured Stalag Luft 4 shortly after the Americans arrived in July and angrily complained to the commandant that conditions were unacceptable, according to the guidelines of the Geneva Convention. Sgt. Reinhard Fahnert's security guards ran the representatives out of the camp at the end of a bayonet. Stalag Luft 6 seemed like a resort compared to Stalag Luft 4.

An American military intelligence report filed in July of 1944 stated that the camp was over-capacity. The Germans said the camp, when completed, would house 6,400 men, but by January

Lager A photographed from the east guard tower. The small building in the row is the latrine servicing the five barracks shown. The low fence in the foreground is the warning fence. Courtesy of Donald Kremper.

of 1945 it housed over 10,000. Red Cross representatives reported to the United States services that the barracks were inadequately ventilated and bathing facilities were not completed. Only one outdoor pump per compound served the prisoners' drinking and bathing needs. Although the report identified the toilet facilities as passable, the men sorely missed their Super Duper privy at Stalag Luft 6. Each compound had two open trenches that seated twenty men, and each barracks had a two-seater, which was the night or lockdown latrine.

The intelligence report stated that food conditions were deplorable and POWs would need clothing shipments before the cold months ahead. Two American doctors worked to keep disease at bay, but failed miserably. Recreation facilities were not present in July when the Red Cross toured the camp, but after their departure, the prisoners fashioned a playing field. While the intelligence-gathering team was concerned with the overall conditions in the prisoner-of-war camp, the men living in the tents at Stalag Luft 4 worried more about getting the barracks completed before the snow flew. Come winter, it would be miserable living in tents.

Meanwhile, the men made the best of it in their tents. Pifer enjoyed the sound of the wind in the pines, which reminded him of home. He could imagine himself in bed at the farm in Pennsylvania. Instead of praying for the compounds to be finished, he focused on hopes that he would be liberated before his birthday in August, but as the thirteenth came and went, no help arrived.

Larry had not celebrated his birthday with his family in over three years. He had been in boot camp on his twentieth birthday. He had been a training instructor in Walla Walla, Washington, on his twenty-first, and now he was in a prisoner-of-war camp on his twenty-second. He couldn't help but speculate where he would be on his next birthday, or whether he would be alive to

View of Lager A through the outer perimeter fence. Note the rolled wire between the fences and the warning fence barely visible behind perimeter fence. On the right side of the photograph, the prisoners of Lager A are playing a game of baseball. Courtesy of Donald Kremper.

observe another year. He shook off that depressing thought and celebrated his birthday by sewing a lighter into his coat.

Earlier that day, he traded some cigarettes for a lighter from one of the Canadian airmen in his compound. And it was a beaut! Larry carefully slit open the pleated vent in the back of his wool coat and the lighter fit inside perfectly. After a few stitches to close the seam, he sat back to admire his work. At least he got a gift on his birthday, he thought to himself.

Slowly, buildings in Compound C and D appeared. Each day more and more men moved from their tents into the newly completed barracks. Gradually, the overcrowded conditions in A and B improved as men moved to C and D. But the men of C and D still had to bathe at the single pump in the yard.

Bathing was a two-man operation. One man pumped two buckets of water. His buddy dashed out of the barracks completely naked. The pump man threw a bucket of water on the naked man, who quickly lathered up his wet body. The pump man then threw the second bucket of water over the soapy prisoner to rinse him off. The naked man streaked across the yard and into the barracks to dress. Then it was the pump man's turn at bathing.

Security in Stalag Luft 4 was extremely tight, compared to that in Stalag Luft 6. A two-hundred-foot clearing separated the forest from the outer perimeter of the camp. Two ten-foot-high fences sandwiched a four-foot rolled barbed-wire fence that surrounded the entire camp. Guards told the prisoners that the outer fence was electrified and no one was daring enough to try and find out. A two-foot wooden warning fence surrounded the inner perimeter of each of the four compounds. Posted signs proclaimed that anyone touching the fence would be shot on sight.

Armed guards with dogs prowled the camp day and night. Guards in towers kept a vigilant eye. If a prisoner aroused suspicion, guards took great pleasure in beating him. All the compounds except A had buildings that were built about two feet off the ground to deter prisoners from digging out. Compound A's buildings were built on slabs of concrete.

The German construction workers quickly finished a bathhouse and latrine in Compound C, but it took them until November to finish the rest of the barracks. The barracks were 40-by-130 feet with ten rooms. Each room was designed to hold sixteen men, but often housed up to thirty-three. The buildings were not weather-proofed and during the winter would prove to be appallingly cold. There were not enough bunks for all the prisoners, so many slept without mattresses on the floor and even on the table. The men used their shoes for pillows. There were

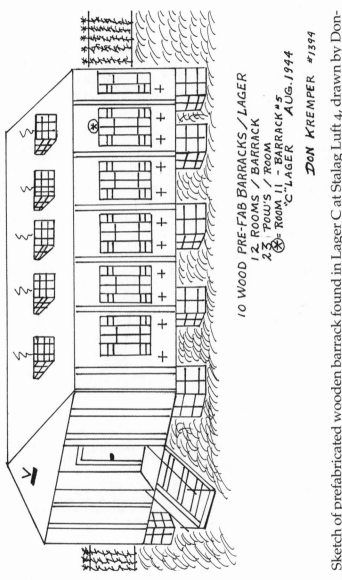

Sketch of prefabricated wooden barrack found in Lager C at Stalag Luft 4, drawn by Donald Kremper. Courtesy of Donald Kremper.

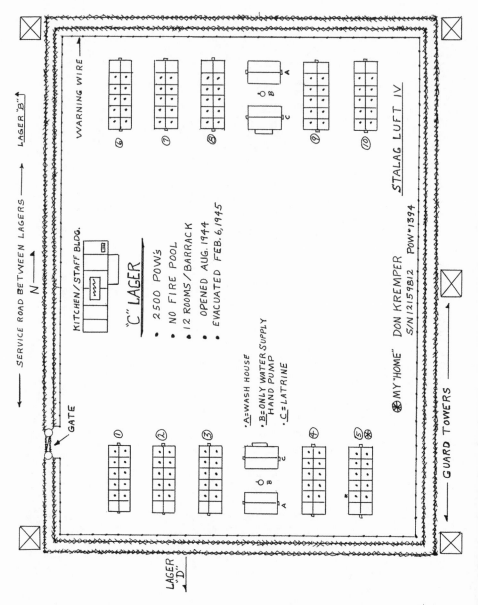

Sketch of Lager C, drawn by Donald Kremper. Courtesy of Donald Kremper.

no storage lockers, so every man wore all his clothes and sewed any personal items into his clothing.

Near the center of the compound were general-purpose buildings used as offices and sleeping rooms for Allied camp leaders, as well as a mess hall or kitchen. Fire pools or shallow concrete ponds filled with water were located near the mess halls in Compounds A and B, but not in C and D. The men of Compound C were glad that they did not have the stagnant, bug-infested pools in their area during the hot months of July and August. The pools exacerbated the unsanitary conditions inside the camp. During the summer, over half the prisoners suffered from diarrhea.

That summer of 1944, while Russian forces moved into Poland, gains were slow in Stalag Luft 4. As summer turned into fall, rain and snow soaked the ground around the unfinished barracks. Leaking tents and mud forced the men inside the barracks, which were already overflowing. During the day, they returned to their tents or wandered around the yard. As the night air cooled, Pifer emptied the little bit of straw that filled the hundred-pound flour sack that he used as a mattress. When it was time to go to bed, he crawled inside the bag and pulled the cord tight. Sealed inside, his body heat kept him warm. Other men in his tent followed suit when they found it was warmer than sleeping on top of the bag. Finally in November, Pifer and the rest of the men living in the tents packed their bedrolls and moved into the completed barracks.

CHAPTER FIFTEEN

LIFE IN CAMP

Pifer joined twenty-seven men in Room 5 of Barrack Four. The ten-by-twelve-foot room seemed palatial after the tents, and joyously the men began dancing a jig on the hard floors of their room. No more sleeping on the damp, cold ground. Now they had a wooden foundation for their bedrolls. It had been a cool, wet fall, which led into a bitterly cold winter. Disease and illnesses ran rampant through the men who had lived in the tents, perhaps things would improve now that they were in barracks.

Even as prisoners of war, airmen and soldiers held to the prescribed hierarchy within the U.S. Army Air Corps. Once they had been in units, squadrons, and bombardment groups; now they followed the principles of military discipline drilled into them from the first day of basic training. However, instead of being assigned a leader, the men elected one individual to command the group while in camp or on forced marches. The men of Barrack Four appointed Sergeant Miller to lead, and then each room chose a second commander. After a leader was accused of doling out unequal food portions, the men of Room 5 elected Pifer as "room führer."

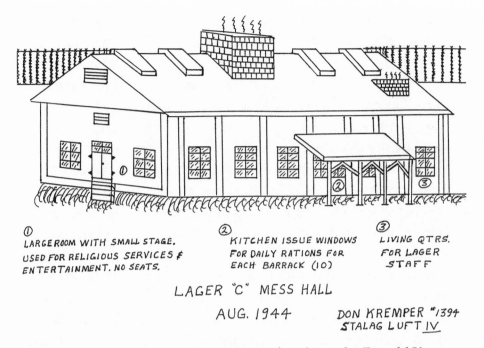

① LARGE ROOM WITH SMALL STAGE. USED FOR RELIGIOUS SERVICES & ENTERTAINMENT. NO SEATS.

② KITCHEN ISSUE WINDOWS FOR DAILY RATIONS FOR EACH BARRACK (10)

③ LIVING QTRS. FOR LAGER STAFF

LAGER "C" MESS HALL

AUG. 1944   DON KREMPER #1394 STALAG LUFT IV

Sketch of Lager C mess hall at Stalag Luft 4, drawn by Donald Kremper. Courtesy of Donald Kremper.

As room leader, Pifer distributed food and parcels, including clothing shipments, to each of the men. At mealtime, the men lined up with their plates and Pifer used his cup to scoop up a portion of sauerkraut, potatoes, stew, or whatever rations were supplied by the German cooks in the mess hall. He took special pains to measure out even portions and scrape out the remnants that clung to his cup. When he divided up the portions of bread, Pifer used a deck of cards to determine who got what piece. He used pairs of cards, lining one set up along the piece of bread for which the men drew a card. They got the portion that matched their card. No one grumbled and everyone felt that he was getting a fair shake.

In a logbook, Pifer made a list of every man in his room, including his prisoner-of-war number and social security number. He kept a detailed account of the clothing that each man possessed. When a Red Cross shipment came in or the German command handed out cast-offs, he consulted his list to see who needed any clothes. After being worn day in and day out for months, POWs' clothes were reduced to mere rags. They were patched from remnants of discarded pants and shirts. In addition to handing out clothes, Pifer adjudicated any problems that arose among the men in Room 5. He was relieved that there were few problems outside of getting food and clothing for his men.

A room and mail! Pifer could hardly believe his luck. After being a prisoner of war for over eight months, he finally received a letter from his sister, Helen, and another from his Aunt Helen.

Mail call was a poignant and emotional time for the men in prisoner-of-war camps. The airmen gathered around a prisoner from the mail work crew with expectant faces. "Kremper, Moeller!" Hands went up and overjoyed men pushed forward to get their precious gift from home. "Pifer!" after a punch on the shoulder and "You lucky dog" from one of the other prisoners, the airman moved away from the group.

With long strides, a grinning Pifer headed back to the privacy of his room to read his letters. Even though he had been writing since September, these were the first letters that he had received since becoming a prisoner of war. He glanced at the date at the top of one letter and then at the postmark. It had taken two months for his sister's letter to arrive. Her newsy message admonished him for not writing. The second letter was from his Aunt Helen. "Boy, what a day!" Pifer thought. Helen was so very happy to hear from him and she wrote that his letter took nine weeks to arrive at her home in Pennsylvania. Could he believe it? He nodded in response. He knew that on average it took two months for letters from home to get to the POWs. Aunt Helen broke the sad news that Larry's cousin, Raymond, had died in April. He was sorry to hear that, for

PRISONER OF WAR POST
KRIEGSGEFANGENENPOST
SERVICE DES PRISONNIERS DE GUERRE

BY AIR MAIL
PAR AVION

AFFIX
6¢
POSTAGE

RANK AND NAME *T/SGT. LAWRENCE E. PIFER*
(CAPITAL LETTERS)   UNITED STATES PRISONER OF WAR.

PRISONER OF WAR No. *3155*
(SEE NOTE ON FLAP)

CAMP NAME AND No. *Stalag Luft III*

SUBSIDIARY CAMP No. *Stalag Luft, 4*

COUNTRY *Germany*

VIA NEW YORK, N. Y.

PRISONER OF WAR POST
KRIEGSGEFANGENENPOST
SERVICE DES PRISONNIERS DE GUERRE

POSTAGE FREE
GEBUHRENFREI
FRANC DE PORT

INDICATE NATIONALITY OF PRISONER OF WAR | U. S. ☐ | BRITISH ☐ | CANADIAN ☐ | OTHER (Specify) ☐

NAME AND GRADE OF PRISONER OF WAR | PRISONER OF WAR No.

ADDRESS

VIA NEW YORK, N. Y.

Prisoner of war post to T/Sgt. Lawrence Pifer. Mail from the United States was sent to Stalag Luft 3 for censorship and then forwarded to Stalag Luft 4 for distribution. Courtesy of Lawrence Pifer.

they had been good friends when they were growing up. His youth seemed ages ago.

Disconsolate airmen returned to the barracks without mail. They pestered roommates to read *their* letters aloud. News from home, anyone's home, was better than nothing at all. Mail was read and reread over and over, filling many a man with the hope that he would eventually make his way back home to the United States. The airmen also felt a sense of pride, knowing that their efforts in the war were keeping loved ones free.

As prisoners, the young men learned the real meaning of the word *free*, and they relished the thought of being free once more. Freedom, for them, would only be achieved at a great cost of life.

Mail traveled through Lisbon, Portugal, and Geneva, Switzerland, before receipt in Germany or in the United States. Prisoners' mail and packages arrived in Stalag Luft 3, near Dresden, Germany, where censors opened each piece. The Germans blacked out portions of letters that they deemed inappropriate. Weeks later, letters and parcels arrived in other Stalag Luft camps for distribution. Sometimes letters arrived so blacked out, a prisoner could only read a sentence or two. If a prisoner was moved to another camp, his letters might or might not be forwarded to him. Censors kept book parcels up to six months before sending them on to their owners.

German orders, passed on to American officials, clearly defined the process for delivering mail and packages to prisoners of war. When he arrived in the first camp, Stalag Luft 6, Pifer's family was notified. Within days of receiving notification that her brother was a prisoner of war, Helen was contacted by the office of the American Provost Marshal General. The Prisoner of War Information Bureau sent a letter and forms that carefully outlined the proper procedures for mailing letters and packages to her brother. The Bureau encouraged Helen and family members to get free letterforms that were available at any United

States Post Office. Form No. 111, a sliver of paper that folded into the shape of an envelope, facilitated censorship, and Helen was assured that her brother would receive it sooner than a typical piece of correspondence.

The Provost Marshal General's Office strongly encouraged correspondents to write only about "personal or family matters" and avoid including any "information of a political or military nature." Families could write an unlimited number of letters to their sons, brothers, and spouses, but they were warned that letters from prisoners were limited.

Once a month, the mail crew distributed mail forms to the prisoners. Officers received three letterforms and four postcards to send home. Noncommissioned officers were supposed to get two letterforms and four postcards. Each man in Pifer's group got only one letterform and two postcards a month. On his single sliver of paper, Larry wrote his sister to tell her that he was alive and well and always waiting for news from home. He reminded her that he did not get enough letterforms to write her often, but hoped to hear from her often. He cautioned her that he was not even sure that the Germans actually mailed all the letters that he wrote. And, by the way, could she send cigarettes?

It was like Christmas when parcels from home began to arrive in camp. Men frantically tore open boxes, laughing and cheering as they pulled out tobacco, toiletries, and games. Even the guards did not spoil their pleasure by slashing their cigarettes in half; at least the guards slashed them from end to end and not across the package! No sealed packages were allowed left unopened.

The POWs wrote letters and postcards begging their families to send chocolates, cigarettes, toiletries, and goods not found in their Red Cross parcels. All the items they asked for were good bargaining chips on the black market. The men bartered for them with each other and with the German guards. While he was interned in Germany, Larry received only two packages of the many sent from home. The Germans pilfered many of the Red Cross packages, so the POWs were sure that guards or censors also confiscated their packages.

Orders from the "Supreme Command of the Wehrmacht" required that commandants of prisoner-of-war camps do everything within their power to prevent rifling of gift shipments for prisoners of war. Any pilfering was to be reported and punished. Although the Wehrmacht explicitly outlined mail distribution procedures, in the end it was up to the individual camp administration to ensure mail delivery. In Stalag Luft 4, Commandant Bombach did not particularly care if the mail was delivered or not. Camp guards ignored Wehrmacht orders and used mail deliveries as psychological leverage. Behavior, good or bad, affected delivery. Several prisoners saw mailbags being fed to the camp incinerator and reported the destruction to Paules and Chapman. Their protests fell on deaf ears, so they enlisted the help of Red Cross representatives. Even then, deliveries were sporadic.

Another way to get around the mail distribution orders was to confiscate items that were considered propaganda. Any package or letters bearing anti-German slogans were impounded so that the offending wrappers could be removed. On the home front, American manufacturers accommodated the German specifications with products specifically packaged slogan-free for the families of POWs and for the Red Cross to mail to the Stalags. The United States Postal Service did not stamp No. 111 letterforms with postmarks considered to be "propaganda" in nature.

In addition, German censors confiscated packages with civilian clothes in them. American officials reminded families again that only military-issue clothing items could be sent to their sons or husbands. Wehrmacht orders instructed that all seized goods be distributed communally in prisoner-of-war camps and not be given to German soldiers. Nevertheless, Pifer and his buddies knew this did not happen. Their guards never seemed to lack American cigarettes and goods.

As the nights grew longer, security guards locked windows and doors between three and four in the afternoon and returned to open them around nine in the morning. In their camp hidden deep within the woods, the airmen could hear battle action to the east. More and more prisoners entering Stalag Luft 4 brought news that the Russian army was pressing into German territory from the east as Allied forces pressed in from the west. Everyone prayed for a speedy liberation. Things were becoming very difficult in camp.

As the battlefront closed in on Stalag Luft 4, food supplies dwindled. The kitchen produced the most unsavory meals imaginable. Soups and mashed potatoes became the mainstay of the prisoners' diet. German cooks used leftovers from the guards' meals, thrown into pots of boiling water. Frequently, the POWs were served fish soup—a mixture of fish bones, heads, and eyes boiled in water. The soup was ready when the eyes floated to the top. When there wasn't any meat, the soup-du-jour became what many of the prisoners referred to as grass soup—a concoction of grass and maggots in boiled water. No seasonings were ever added to the pots.

Slim rations of coke, coal, and wood for their stoves often meant cold and undercooked meals. The camp kitchen tried to buy meat and vegetables from local farms. Fresh produce and meat that came into camp during the summer months were reduced to a trickle during the winter. Farmers did not want to part with their winter stores. They had families to feed until the next growing season. They adamantly refused to supply meat and vegetables for prisoners of war, but agreed to supply enough to feed German guards. Occasionally, a farmer hauled in a horse carcass to sell to the camp POW kitchen. On other occasions, animals were killed during a military skirmish and guards hauled them into camp, providing the prisoners' kitchen with horse, dog, and chicken. Hunger gnawed away at the resolve of the prisoners and morale dropped drastically until one day a plane dropped from the sky.

Skimming the tops of the trees, four German fighters buzzed the prison camp and banked sharply. Within minutes they returned tipping their wings left and right. For several days, the fighters dropped in to taunt the grounded flyers with their acrobatic moves. Then one day a single fighter returned to buzz one last time over the treetops. His left wing dipped too low and the plane spun around like a top before crashing into the forest. A loud explosion rocked the camp. A ball of fire shot into the air. Laughter and cheers went up, but quickly quieted as angry guards sent a volley of shots into the compounds. Being fired at did not dampen the glee of the American and British airmen. There was one less German hotshot for the B-17s to worry about.

Many of the men in camp set traps to capture wayward birds, rabbits, even rats. Starvation drove many of the prisoners to eat things they would not touch under different circumstances. Rats ran rampant in camp and were easier to catch than birds or rabbits.

One afternoon, Pifer spied a hole at the corner of the barracks. When he crouched for a closer inspection, another prisoner joined him. "What do you have?" "A rat hole, I think." They decided they would take turns watching the hole to see if they could capture a rat. No rodent was forthcoming.

Even inside the barracks, rats engaged in continuous combat with the men of Compound C. Shortly after falling asleep, Pifer felt a large rat running across his face. Now wide-awake, he lay quietly, waiting for the rat's next mad dash. Holding his shoe, a German-made hobnailed boot, the hunter patiently waited.

When the rat prepared to run across his face again, Pifer struck, hitting himself in the eye. A high-pitched squeak squeezed into his left ear. "Damn! missed it." Minutes passed before the varmint dashed again. The boot fell again. A volley of cursing rained on the sleepers around Pifer. A couple of roommates stirred and asked what was up. "Nothing. Nothing," he said. "Just a damn rat." With his eye throbbing, Pifer rolled over and went back to sleep.

In the morning, the men in Room 5 whooped with laughter when Pifer described his night escapade. A slow grin sliced across his face until it met the slit of his eye, which was so swollen it hurt to grin. Pifer looked as if he had been in a fight with a boxer and had lost! In the barrack's small mirror made from the end of a tin can, he could see the outline of the boot's nails around his black and blue eye.

Using cigarettes and clothes, starving men bargained for canned goods with their fat and rosy-cheeked guards. As the days turned into months, the POWs worried that they would starve before the ground forces freed them. Many fell ill from lack of nutrients. Weak with hunger, men slept more and more during the day. Some worried that their buddies would never ever wake up again. Reluctantly, prisoners who had carefully hoarded their Red Cross parcels shared their meager stores with those who had impulsively gulped down their own in a few days. Groups of men combined ingredients to make a meal. The half-rations that they endured during the first few weeks in camp was a feast compared to what they endured now. Food supplies trickled into camp.

When food rations were cut for the guards as well, the giant one, called "Big Stoop" by the prisoners, became meaner and meaner. Six feet eight inches tall, the German towered over most of the Americans. When new prisoners came into the compound, Big Stoop picked on them unmercifully. He took pleasure in

Four American airmen lying in a snow bank during the winter of 1944. Note that three of the men are wearing their flight jackets. Author's collection.

boxing the ears of an unsuspecting prisoner. One bewildered airman did not understand the order to get back. As Big Stoop bellowed *"Zurück,"* he grabbed the American by the collar of his coat and shoved him back, eventually knocking him to the ground. After the third time, the American realized what the German wanted and moved quickly out of the way.

The winter of 1944–45 turned out to be one of the coldest on record. In the morning and evening, all that the prisoners could hear was the crunch of their boots on the snow. No one talked because faces were burrowed into collars to keep tender noses from freezing. Counters tallied the men and quickly headed back into their warm rooms in the Vorlager. Hands froze to the water pump; even fastidious airmen no longer washed up. It was too cold.

The refuse in the latrines was too frozen for the Russian POW latrine crew to clean out with vacuum pumps. Bitter winds blew down from the frozen north and whipped in between cracks in the walls of the barracks. As the temperatures dropped below zero, the cold air inside the barracks felt to the men like the inside of a meat locker. Pifer put on all the clothes he owned underneath his coat and wrapped the two German blankets he was issued around his shoulders. He just could not get warm.

The Geneva Convention guidelines mandated that each prisoner was to receive an allotment of one brick of coke or coal per day. In actuality, each prisoner got one per week to heat his stove. Pifer had been around the coal mines of central Pennsylvania long enough to know that the briquettes that they were getting were neither coal nor charcoal.[1] It appeared that the bricks were made of coal dust mixed with clay to form a briquette. The amount of clay in the product made it hard for them to light the fire in the stove. To make matters worse, the guards became stingier and stingier with the dole of matches.

Once every week or two, the camp administration called in a sewage work crew to clean out the pits. Russian prisoners made up the work crew. They lowered a pipe from their heat-powered vacuum into the sewage pit. Gas in the pit filled the pipe. A worker lit the gas with a match. Voom! Lighting the gas caused an explosion that sucked the waste out of the pit and into a gigantic wooden barrel on a wagon. The Russians knew that matches were a scarce commodity in camp and often passed them to prisoners by faking dud strikes.

"No light. No light." Shaking his head, the Russian walked away to join his friends at the front of the wagon. Pifer mentally marked the spot and waited. Shortly after the wagon left, he sauntered over to the spot, bent down to "tie" his bootlace and pocketed the matches. The Russians pulled the wagon through the gate and into the next compound. Once the wagon was loaded, they hauled their cargo of waste to a dump some distance from the camp and shoveled it on to the field to be plowed under next spring. When the pits were frozen solid, the work crew hacked at it with shovels and stacked a flat-bed wagon with chunks of smelly muck.

Just before Christmas a rumor spread through camp that a shipment of ice skates was coming. Elated young men braved the knee-deep snow and sub-zero temperatures to fashion an ice skating rink on the recreation grounds. They used window shutters as shovels to push the snow around and form a bank for the rink. Pumping water from two wells, the men formed a bucket brigade to haul water to the banked pool. It didn't take long for the water to freeze solid. Some were too impatient to wait for the skates to arrive and began to slide around on their boots, often ending up on their rear ends. The anticipated ice equipment never arrived, or if it did, it was confiscated. However, for a few days and weeks, the prisoners enjoyed making their ice rink and dreamt of gliding across it on their yet-to-arrive blades.

As the holiday season drew nearer, the men behind the barbed wire turned their thoughts more and more to loved ones. Larry wrote a letter to his sister, Helen, on December 12th asking for cigarettes and tobacco for the pipe she sent him. He really enjoyed the pipe. It took a little bit of practice to learn how to tamp the tobacco into the bowl and light it. If he packed it too tight, it was difficult to light the tobacco and keep it lit. When it went out, a trickle of juice ran down the stem and into the back of his throat, gagging him. Eventually, he learned how to measure out the right amount of tobacco for it to light and stay lit. Now Larry felt like a professional pipe smoker. The problem was getting tobacco and matches to keep him supplied. He also asked her to tell an old sweetheart to "give it up" and not write any more.

Like many of the relatives of men fighting in World War II, Ivan Pifer signed up with tobacco companies to have shipments of tobacco products sent to his son. In the winter of 1944 and 1945,

Larry began to receive them. Not a demonstrative man, Ivan found it difficult to write—in fact, he wrote only one letter to Larry during his imprisonment. It was easier for him to express his affection for his son by sending shipments of tobacco.

With thoughts of Christmas came memories of family dinners and celebrations. Lying around the room, the young Americans reminisced about the special foods that their grandmothers, mothers, sisters, and wives cooked and baked for the holidays. To pass time, they made a game of it. "Let's see how many different types of pies we can name!" "Pifer, you keep a list of this."

So putting pencil to paper, their room leader made a list of their favorite pies. "Boston crème pie. Mincemeat!" As they called out custard, berry, and cream pies, the hungry men pictured familiar kitchens warm and fragrant with baking pies and the list grew. Men with a sweet tooth craved a variety of candies. Like children who dreamt of sugarplums the night before Christmas, they envisioned chocolate-covered cherries and peanuts, bonbons, jellybeans, peanut clusters, coconut clusters, and candy bars. They decided that a gumdrop, peppermint, or chocolate drop would tantalize their taste buds for hours if they only had one! Many a man argued that his mom's homemade fudge was the best in the world.

Food occupied their thoughts a good deal of their waking hours during the winter months. In his notebook, Pifer carefully penciled in tiny script the numerous candy bars the men called out. Someone shouted, "When I get home I'm going to work for Hershey!" Laughter erupted. Even though their stomachs shrank, their desire for goodies did not.

During the Christmas preparations, the men shared stories of Christmases at home in Georgia, New Hampshire, Colorado, and across the United States. Sing-a-longs became a favorite prison activity. When they couldn't remember the words to a carol, the men just made up the words or went from room to

room searching for someone who did remember the words.
Instead of feeling lifted in spirit, some young men became angry.
They began to question whether there really was a God, and if
there was, how He could allow this horrible war to continue.
While some accepted counseling from fellow inmates, others
turned from God and friends.

Many men found comfort and solace in prayer and attempted
to follow religious tradition by celebrating the Sabbath. While
the German command did everything possible to discourage
religious celebrations and gatherings, the YMCA worked stead-
fastly to supply those who desired a Bible and hymnal. Catho-
lics, Protestants, and American Jews attempted to carry on their
traditions and pray for freedom.

During the Advent season, those who had not attended any
previous religious activities now came forward to listen to
words of encouragement or to sing familiar tunes traditionally
heard during the holy season. Services were an opportunity for
the men to gather together. Cautious security guards kept a
close watch on the prisoners and posted men at the door of the
assembly to listen in, never quite believing a religious service
was not a meeting to calculate a break-out.

After the holidays, a feeling of despair and depression haunted
the prisoners. They struggled to keep warm and feed their under-
nourished bodies. Fighting in the east continued, but many gave
up hope that it would reach their camp. Rumors that they might
be liberated began soon after the arrival of the New Year in 1945.
Prisoners from other camps started to crowd into Stalag Luft 4.
A glimmer of hope brightened the POWs' days once again.

The airmen prayed that the Russian troops moving toward
Berlin would soon liberate them. Those hopes were dashed
when guards taunted them with threats, saying that the high
command planned to kill them all before the Germans fell back.
Hitler toyed with the idea of gathering the prisoners of war to

form a shield around German cities, but was talked out of this by his advisors. From his bunker, the Führer ordered SS General Gottlob Berger, chief of POWs, to kill them all. Allied spies working in the countryside heard the news and tried to get arms to POWs with little success. In the end, Stalag Luft 4's commandant decided to hold onto his prisoners to use them as bargaining chips in the event that he and his German troops were captured. Prisoners in other camps were not so lucky and died at the hands of their captors.

Because of the frigid winds circling in and around the buildings, most men stayed inside behind closed shutters during the day. Crowding and improper ventilation caused diseases to spread among the men weakened by lack of food and warmth. Prisoners who fell seriously ill were taken to the Vorlager hospital with its 132 beds. American and British doctors lived in a building adjacent to the hospital. At night, they were forced to leave their patients unattended. Inside the compounds, dispensaries tended to as many of the men as they could. Medics treated comrades. Because of unsanitary conditions, common ailments included athlete's foot, lice, skin rashes, and swollen joints. Colds, pneumonia, and frostbite became frequent complaints as below-zero temperatures blanketed northern Europe. Pifer felt fortunate that he had a strong constitution.

The only time he had been really ill was when he got a severe sinus infection. It blinded him. He could hardly sit up, and even walking was excruciating. The movement jolted his head and thunderbolts of pain stopped him in his tracks. He vomited and vomited. The pain caused him to become temporarily blind. He didn't know what to do. He was so miserable.

Wondering if heat would help break up the mass of infection, Pifer traded his birthday lighter for seven hundred cigarettes. For days, he lay in his bunk lighting cigarettes and searing his forehead with the burning end. When the cigarette butt shrank, he lit the next cigarette with it. He could hear crackling and popping inside his head as the mass began to break up. The treatment burned a scar across his forehead that gradually calloused. Standing at roll call one morning, he looked wistfully at the warning fence. He contemplated making a run for it. "All I have to do is hit the fence and they would take me out of my misery," he thought. In the end, Pifer endured the pain and after three weeks the congestion in his sinuses broke loose. His headaches went away but it took months before the scars from the burn disappeared.

Pifer was otherwise healthy during his camp sojourn. He was luckier than most of the guys and was able to help with some of the sick men in his barracks. When carpenters hung bunk beds on the walls of the barracks in Compound C in January, the sick were moved off the cold floor. Any extra bunks were filled with the rest of the airmen as space allowed.

Typhoid was common in camp. Providentially, typhoid serum was delivered in January and doctors set about inoculating all the prisoners. Soon after, a trainload of sick and wounded left camp on January 28th, headed for Stalag Luft 1 at Barth, Germany.

As January turned to February, the battle between the Germans and Russians came as close as Kiefheide. The Russian artillery shelled the railroad depot. Another trainload of men headed to a hospital at Nürenberg, Germany, as soon as the tracks were cleared. Camp leaders Paules and Chapman told their men that the commandant was negotiating with the Russian army commander. Bombach was willing to turn over the prisoners to the Russians. While some POWs rejoiced, others were cautiously optimistic. They wondered why the Russians would want to worry about prisoners when they were pushing through to Berlin.

In the early hours of February 6th, guards roused prisoners and told them they must get ready to march at once. Everyone fell out. Barracks emptied. The boots of over ten thousand men

Evacuation of prisoners from Stalag Luft 4, February 6, 1945.
Courtesy Donald Kremper.

trampled the fourteen inches of snow that lay on the ground
inside the camp. Ice crystals hung suspended in the air. It was
too cold to snow—or to speak.

The stamping of boots packed the snow even harder. The
prisoners formed a long line four across on the recreation
grounds. Compound A filed out and past the storage warehouse
in the Vorlager. Guards opened the doors of the warehouse
and passed two Red Cross parcels and a blanket to each man.

Compound B, then C, filed out of their wired fortresses and past the warehouse.

Pifer quickly grabbed his boxes and held them close. It was the most food he had seen in over a year and he was not about to lose hold of it. The Lager logbook thumped against his thigh. It was safely hidden. The flyers carried their food and possessions in homemade backpacks or rucksacks. Bedrolls were fastened to their packs or thrown over their shoulders. "Halt!" Guards divided their prisoners into groups of two to three hundred. Pifer and Moeller formed a quad with two more men. This time the Germans abandoned the idea of chaining their prisoners. There were too many men and not enough hand-cuffs or chains. In step, the column moved out of camp in the early hours of February 6, 1945.

CHAPTER SIXTEEN

THE BLACK MARCH

A frozen fog muffled the sounds in camp. Icy puffs spewed forth when anyone spoke or shouted an order. The ice-covered curtain parted as the column of men marched out of Stalag Luft 4 and turned onto the snow-covered road leading to Kiefheide. The guards did not even bother to close the gates to the camp. Only a small group of prisoners and a doctor remained behind. They were too sick to move and the doctor would not leave his charges.

A large contingent of guards hurried the flyers through the pine forest. Snow hung on the trees. The evergreens grew so thick that very little snow accumulated underneath their bowers. German trucks moving in and out of Stalag Luft had cleared a track into camp, making the march through the snow easier than the prisoners had expected. A light snow began to fall on drifts along the road that were already fourteen to twenty inches high. Pifer was glad that he had his long winter coat and that it hung nearly to his ankles. He considered himself lucky to have received new G.I. shoes to replece the German hob-nailed boots. He pulled down the earflaps on his knit cap and concentrated on keeping pace with his group.

Before they left camp, the formation leader said the march to Stargard was approximately a three-day hike. Free from the constraints of the compound and barbed wire, Pifer felt exhilarated. The brisk pace set by the guards kept them warm for most of the day. At the end of the second day, the prisoners began to wonder if they indeed were headed to Stargard. None of the signs they passed on the road indicated it. When they stopped for the night inside a barn, Pifer pulled off his boots and found that his toes had pushed clean through his socks. Pulling the ends of the socks well past his toes, he tucked the excess underneath them and tried to shove his feet back into his boots. Many prisoners complained about blisters, aching joints, and wet shoes. The guards did not fare any better. Many of them were padding their boots with extra socks and trying to dry them out. After the winter months and no strenuous activity, most of the prisoners and guards were out of shape for such a long march.

The seventeen-kilometer march soon lengthened to twenty, then twenty-five. In another time and place, the men would have enjoyed a leisurely hike through the forests and hills of eastern Germany, but in the dead of winter, and a bitterly cold one at that, it was an ordeal.

On the road, refugees pushed carts and prams containing all their worldly belongings. Babies cried. Despair showed on the faces of the fleeing travelers. Among them were farmers and their families with all their belongings piled into a wagon, which was pulled by a team of horses. Some wagons had a milk cow tied to the back. Germans who had once lived in East Prussia, Poland, and other lands were fleeing their homes and returning there.

Drained beyond human endurance, elders stumbled and collapsed to the ground. Family members rushed to pick them up before the marching column of prisoners trampled them. People were headed west, betting that their fate would be brighter with the Allied troops than with the storming Russians from the east.

A cold, steady rain soaked the men on Valentine's Day. They had been on the road for over a week now. Using a blanket as a shroud to keep the rain off his shoulders, Pifer turned inward to his private thoughts. "When will we stop for the night?" The soaking blanket soon began to weigh down his head and his chin fell to his chest. One foot forward, then the next. Mechanically, he marched onward. It was near midnight when the guards ordered them off the road.

The airmen slipped and slid down the sides of a ditch and up the other side to a pasture. There would be no cover from the rain tonight. In the early hours of the morning, the drizzle subsided. At dawn, the cold, wet men began to stir. A leg or an arm moved and muddy specters of two or four bodies rose from the field. They paused to relieve themselves. Combine partners struggled up the sides of the ditch to the road and joined the formation.

Within a couple days, the lowlands gave way to marshlands where the Oder River emptied into Stettin Bay. Licks of white foam rippled across the surface of the bay. A small boat waited for them at the pier. The boat sank into the swells as guards and prisoners filled the hold. It carried them across the bay and into the small port city of Stettin.

The port was already busy with men loading and unloading ships. The prisoners disembarked from the boat and fell into formation. They skirted the business district and entered the residential portion of the city. Silence hung heavy over the stone houses. Army shoes and boots clattered on the stone streets leading away from the boat landing and the city. Here and there a few lights burned in bedrooms and kitchens where early risers dressed and sat with their hot cups of coffee before beginning their workday. Curtains twitched as residents looked to see who was marching through the town.

The column marched west from Stettin toward Lauenbūrg at the River Elbe, passing Berlin to the south. It was difficult for the men to track their route because their direction seemed to change daily. Occasionally, the group drew near to the banks of the Elbe on their southern route, but it wasn't until they reached Lauenbūrg that the column boarded a ferry to cross the river.

Section by section, guards loaded their prisoners onto the ferry, which moved slowly across the river. The ferry with its heavy load of tired muddied bodies left a *V* in its wake. On the other side, Pifer watched the ferry move back and forth until all the airmen were together. Once again, in formation, he turned with the rest of the men and marched down the road.

The Red Cross parcels distributed in camp were now gone. Food rations from the kitchen truck, which followed the column, were almost gone. Days passed when the men had nothing to fill their stomachs. In the first thirty days of the march, guards handed out less than one loaf of bread to each prisoner. At first, the Germans threatened to shoot any prisoner caught trading for food with refugees or peasants on the road. But when all their food was gone, the guards became as desperate as their captives.

At times, the men went without food for five days. Pifer tried to ignore the hunger pains that wracked his body, but it became impossible. He needed more than a sugar cube and a third of a cigarette to survive. He cut off a length of his coat and traded it for a loaf of bread. The peasant walked away with the wool "stole" for a wife or daughter.

When there wasn't any soup to serve, the cooks served potatoes they bought from farmers. When the spuds were gone, men foraged in dormant farm fields and woods for vegetables or bark and leaves to fill their growling stomachs. In farm country, they all—Americans and Germans alike—scavenged what they could from the fields. Prisoners dug with their bare hands in the frozen earth, looking for vegetables. In many cases, all they ended up with were torn and bleeding fingertips. Conditions became so desperate that guards forced one farmer to give over the slop he mixed for his sows.

The refugees suffered as well. The refugees scraped the snow off pastures as best they could to allow their animals to forage, but it was never enough for the animals to survive. First one horse and then another died; farmers and their families pushed or pulled their wagons. The carcasses were cut up and thrown into the wagon bed. When the weight in the wagon was too much for them to be able to move it, families threw out their belongings.

Occasionally, an American or Allied fighter flew over and strafed a cow or horse in a pasture near the marching column. The prisoners never knew for sure if the pilot recognized them as starving allied POWs and killed the animal for them, or if he simply killed it for target practice, or out of spite. It did not matter. The entire column stopped for the day and ate. Guards ordered prisoners to gather firewood for campfires to melt snow for coffee and barbecue the meat. It didn't seem so bad sleeping out in the open those nights. With a full stomach and rested limbs, it was just another day on the road.

The days and weeks ran together. The men marched until they dropped. The guards were just as weary from the continuous marching and didn't want to march any more than their prisoners did. They were tired and wanted to go home to their loved ones. For some, this was not a war of their choosing and it had gone on too long.

At night, the column sought shelter and many times found barns or buildings already filled with other prisoners or refugees. They turned and marched until they found somewhere else to stay or slept in the open. All they did was march, eat (if lucky), and sleep.

The column weaved first east, then west along the roads of central Germany. Rain and snow soaked the men. The wet wool blanket was a dead weight on Pifer's shoulders. No matter how he carried his blanket, whether over a shoulder or around his neck, the pain in his shoulders and back became unbearable. Moeller would come to his aid and carry the blanket until the pain in Pifer's shoulders eased. On other days, Pifer would carry his combine buddy's blanket for him. Sharing the burden of war and then prison life was the only thing that kept most of the men alive.

At night when the prisoners were allowed to stop early enough to scrounge for food, Moeller and Pifer, worked as a team to get a fire started and prowl for food. Moeller got a light from someone and directed Pifer to gather firewood while he got their tender going.

As Pifer trudged through the woods near the clearing gathering broken limbs, he saw a turkey enter a woodsy heap. Upon closer inspection, Pifer realized that someone had formed an apiary out of tree boughs. The bees were going in and out, but the prisoner did not see the bird come back out. So he sat down to wait.

When Pifer did not come back with the firewood, Moeller went in search of his buddy. Boy, was he pissed. "If you aren't going to help me with the fires, then damn it you aren't getting any of the potatoes!" Recently, Pifer had had an opportunity to steal some potatoes at a farm where they stopped for the night. He and Moeller hid the potatoes in their clothes and carefully rationed a portion out for each day's meal. Moeller gathered up a nearby pile of wood and stomped off with it, furious that Pifer had not even bothered to respond.

Patiently, Pifer waited and waited for the turkey. He felt sure that the bird went in to lay her eggs in that sheltered spot. In a little while, the turkey appeared. She stopped and sensed Pifer's presence, but when he did not move and stayed as still as the trees around him, she moved on. Quickly, before any of the others foraging for wood saw the turkey leave her nest, Pifer dived into the apiary and pulled out three eggs.

He hurried back to Moeller who was now frying some potatoes in a can over the fire he had made. Moeller, still miffed, ignored his arrival. When Pifer walked up and squatted down next to him, Moeller told him to get lost. Pifer apologized for not bringing in the wood, but said, "I have something good to go with those potatoes." He pulled the eggs out from under his coat and suggested that they would sure be good fried in among the potatoes. Moeller forgave him and they had one of the best meals they had eaten in a long time. They relished their meal of eggs and potatoes, because they knew plenty of days would pass without anything to eat.

On the road, they met other columns of men from Stalag Luft 4 who were as weak and weary as their own contingent. The once healthy young flyers, their hope hanging only by a thin thread, began to unravel as the pounds slid off their forms. Pifer wondered if they would ever be liberated before they starved to death. He was sure that if he allowed himself to weep, he would never be able to stop.

The ragtag group passed abandoned household goods. Occasionally, they passed a frozen body. Refugees on the road dropped books, bags of clothes, and kitchen utensils, too tired to care anymore. Men dropped out of the line to rifle through the bags, looking for food or warm clothes. The guards did not stop them; they often joined in the search.

The refugees headed west and in the same direction as the POWs, away from the advancing Russians. The Germans were terrified of the Russians. When German troops marched into Russia earlier in the war, they exterminated Russian Jews and then turned on the citizen populace, murdering millions. Now in retaliation, the Russian army advanced into Germany killing, looting, and raping. Neither did the Americans want to fall into Russian hands, even now.

Occasionally, the column joined German troops moving along the roads. Mixing with enemy soldiers frightened the captive American flyers. They would rather hide among the refugees. When a British Typhoon or American P-51 fighter saw soldiers, it would swoop down and spray the line with machine-gun fire.

Pifer watched as a Typhoon swept in low and headed right for him. "Well, if you are going to hit me, hit me good and don't cripple me." The bullets punctured flesh and tore at the ground. Men dropped, screaming and crying out in pain. Pifer turned and watched the fighter climb higher and higher into the clouds. He wondered if he would ever be released from this hell on earth. At times, Allied planes flew over groups of wandering POWs, unknowingly strafing their own men.

At the end of February, a Red Cross truck on its way to make a delivery at a POW camp stopped on the road to distribute food parcels. Red Cross volunteers handed a box to each combined pair. Having distributed its entire load, the truck turned and headed back to its point of operations. With boxes in hand, the prisoners made their way to an abandoned barnyard to eat their feast.

Men collapsed onto the ground and tore open their boxes. While they reveled at their luck in meeting the Red Cross truck, an Allied fighter plane flew over. The men were too busy eating to cheer. They heard the engine before they spied the plane circling back toward them. Suddenly, machine-gun fire splattered the ground. A shell dropped into the group and exploded.

Pifer leapt up in surprise and ran for cover. They were being shelled and bombed by their own allies again! One minute, they were enjoying their parcels, like kids opening Christmas packages, and the next they were being strafed. Seven prisoners died that day.

Eventually, the column from Compound C came to a railroad depot where a long line of rail cars waited. The men scrambled into the cars, looking forward to riding instead of marching. Despite the number of cars on the siding, they were quickly filled beyond capacity. The prisoners would have to stand. It was two days before the train lurched forward out of the rail yard and headed west into Germany.

Exhaustion and illness overcame many within the rail cars. Men collapsed. No man worried that he would fall and injure himself. The crowded airmen supported the sick until their legs gave out and they slowly sank to the floor. The guards had not made any provisions for the men to relieve themselves, so they used their klim cans (empty milk cans) to urinate in and dumped them out through the slats of the rail car. Since most suffered from dysentery or some other intestinal ailment and had no pail to defecate in, the stench in the boxcar became almost intolerable. The men were past feeling embarrassed as excrement ran down their legs and pooled at their feet.

Even during the two-day wait in the rail yard, the guards did not let the prisoners out of their crowded cars to eat, sleep, or relieve themselves. In 1947, a doctor testifying in front of the United States War Crimes Board declared that German guards imposed cruel and unnecessary treatment with regard to that rail yard incident. He reported that a pump, a short distance from the train and in the railroad yard, had a good supply of water. The guards used it to bathe and drink from in clear view of the filthy and thirsty prisoners. The guards slept in the depot and walked the tracks, keeping their distance from the smelly cars.

On March 30 or Good Friday, the train reached its destination—Stalag 11B. This camp was an international prisoner-of-war camp near Fallingbostel, between Hanover and Hamburg. The camp housed approximately seventy-five thousand men representing all branches of the service. Men from India, Russia, Mongolia, Italy, France, Britain, Canada, and America crowded into 11B.

The column from Stalag Luft 4 headed to the showers to be deloused. Pifer and his group removed their clothes and handed them to a work crew. They stood shivering in the cold until it was their turn at the showers. Slowly, the prisoners filed into the shower room. Two to three men surrounded each shower-head. Pifer and his two shower mates scrubbed as quickly as possible when the water came on. Three minutes later, the water was turned off and they returned once again to the larger room in the bathhouse. After almost two months on the road, the three-minute shower hardly washed the top layer of dirt off their bodies. Pifer hopped around to keep warm and wished he had a towel to dry himself off or wrap around his naked body. Finally, after what seemed to be an eternity, a work crew returned to the bathhouse with the prisoners' clothes.

While the POWs were showering, their clothes were taken to the ovens. A delousing work crew used a row of dry brick ovens to steam piles of uniforms in order to kill the lice lurking in the fabric. After a five-minute steaming session, the clothes were carried into the bathhouse and returned to their owners. The warm clothes were a welcome sight to the shivering airmen. The men got a chance to shave, but not to get a haircut. Still, clean and warm once again, Pifer felt almost rejuvenated.

Spurts of warm weather hinted that spring was on its way, but suddenly a cold snap hit the region. During the march, Pifer had traded his coat for food. Now he had to find himself a jacket for sale. For the price of seven cigarettes and five matches, he bought one from a Canadian in camp. With a jacket for warmth, Pifer could afford to trade an extra shirt for food.

The prisoners watched as a Red Cross truck arrived from Lübeck and backed into a warehouse. The French commander of the compound that Pifer's group was quartered in checked off the invoice and the truck pulled out of camp. The new arrivals felt sure that they would be included in the distribution of the parcels and were dismayed when the commander distributed boxes only to his own men. It appeared the French prisoners in Stalag 11B were not willing to share their packages with the starving Americans and Brits. Pifer peeled off his shirt and began to look for a willing buyer.

One prisoner offered him some bran. It was coarse bran used to feed cows and pigs. First Pifer tried to eat the raw bran. It was bitter. When it proved unpalatable, he tried to cook it like oatmeal. A Yugoslav prisoner watched as Pifer stirred his meal and began to shake his head. When Pifer took a bite of the cooked porridge, the Yugoslav shook his head even more. Pifer spit out his mouthful. It had become even more bitter with cooking. Then Pifer realized that the Yugoslav was trying to tell him that eating the bran was out of the question. Obviously, the Slav had already tried it.

Longing to stay in one place for more than a night or two, Pifer and his friends were disappointed when soldiers of the Wehrmacht arrived to escort them out of camp. Early on April 1st, Easter Sunday, the men of Compound C reported to roll call.

These German guards were obviously rookies at marching. They lined up with large packs on their backs and belts of ammunition for the pistols and the rifle they carried. "Get a load of these guys!" Chuckles and laughter broke out among the prisoners.

As the column marched through the gate to the camp, the airmen began to chant, "Super man, super man!" They set off on a pace that had the guards doing double-time. As the day wore on, the guards began to tire and lag behind. The column marched faster and once again chanted "super man." The guards ran to keep up. By the end of the day, the Germans staggered and collapsed to the ground when setting up camp for the night.

The next day, when the column fell into formation, their guards carried only a lunch, canteen of water, and a rifle. They learned quickly.

When the column left Stalag 11B, it headed east once again. As the days passed, the guards allowed their prisoners to rest more often, even lying over in shelters on rainy days. Leaves had begun to form on the trees. Tulips, daffodils, and crocuses were beginning to bloom. As the temperatures rose, lice, crabs, and scabies returned to trouble the men.

Sitting along the road during a break, Pifer ran his thumbnail down the seam of his pantleg to scrape away the lice congregated in the fold. He pulled his lice-covered nail away and scraped it in the dirt. He repeated the process until he had raked most of the pests off his pants. He decided to clean his shirt and coat later. No amount of plucking or scraping of clothes could remove all the vermin, and the prisoners hoped they would soon get another opportunity to visit a prisoner-of-war camp for delousing. Some food would be nice too. But for now, it was time to move on. Pifer stood and joined his buddies.

Starvation prompted desperate action in some. One night when the exhausted column crammed inside a farmer's barn, an angry roar went up. A guard, his face infused with anger, spun on the prisoners with his gun drawn. He ordered the prisoners to line up. Screaming abuse, he pointed to every tenth man and separated him from the rest of the column.

A fearful lump rose in Pifer's throat as he joined the small group of men. Orders for the guards to form up did not quell his fears. Terror coursed through his limbs when a firing squad of German soldiers lined up thirty feet away.

The snarling guard halted in front of the main group. Suddenly, he was quiet. A threatening silence surrounded the weary, filthy prisoners. Ominously, in hushed tones, the guard spoke,

"You have fifteen minutes to replace the stolen bread from my pack or I shoot these men." He waved his arm toward the firing squad and its singled-out prey.

Pifer's heart sank. What if they had eaten the bread? What if it was one of the guards who stole the bread instead of one of the airmen? A guard would not care if a few prisoners were shot. He seethed inside at the insanity of the situation that he had no control over. "I've survived hell only to stand in some farmyard in Germany to be shot for a damn piece of bread. And horrible, tasteless bread at that!"

With their heads turned in embarrassment, and in fear, the milling group of prisoners peeked at the line of prisoners lined up in front of the German firing squad. At the end of fifteen minutes, the longest fifteen minutes in Pifer's life, the column returned to formation. The guard strode over to his pack and opened the flap. He stood silently for a minute with his back to the group that had just reformed. Pifer cursed under his breath. The guard slowly turned and quietly stared at the prisoners singled out to be shot.

The order to fall out was given. Fortunately for the men before the firing squad, the bread ration was replaced in the guard's pack. The prisoners, who had endured agonizing minutes in front of the column, glanced at each other nervously. Time stopped. The two groups stared at one another. The singled-out men stood planted to the ground and wondered if they could ever trust anyone again. Someone beside Pifer swore and stepped forward. The spell was broken.

With weak knees, Larry joined his combine partner and collapsed to the ground. He thanked God that he was not shot. With a heavy heart, he realized that, despite the militant "team" mentality drilled into him, in the end every man is on his own when it came to survival. And, if given the chance, he would kill, with his bare hands, the fool who stole the ration of bread.

On the road once again, men, too weak and sick to continue, dropped out of the straggling formation. At first, friends carried each other until they could go no farther, but eventually no one had the strength to carry anyone but himself. Not only were POWs suffering from extreme physical exertion and hunger, now they were growing weak with disease caused by starvation and unsanitary conditions. The men began to suffer from typhus fever, dysentery, pneumonia, diphtheria, and pellagra. After they drank water from ditches and streams, dysentery spread through the column. It wasn't unusual to see one man drinking from a ditch and downstream another man relieving himself in it.

There were some reports that when an ill prisoner dropped out of formation a guard fell out and a shot was heard. Then the guard returned alone. Pifer never witnessed these incidents, but did not question the truthfulness of the stories.

A wagon followed the group picking up stragglers, allowing a few of the sick and injured an opportunity to rest or sleep. The wagon became so full that when one got on another had to get off. When a horse became exhausted or lame and replacements were not available, prisoners pulled the wagon. When the wagon entered a town, guards took the seriously ill prisoners to a local hospital for care. Rarely did the hospital accept such cases. It was already filled with their own people and administrators could not care less about the health of a prisoner of war.

While the prisoners struggled to survive their forced march in Germany, in the United States those closest to President Franklin Delano Roosevelt worried about the pale, gaunt man who struggled to bring the war to an end and his boys home. During a respite to his beloved Warm Springs, Georgia, FDR died on April 12, 1945. The men who had followed their supreme commander's order into combat and were now prisoners of war did not learn of his demise until some weeks later.

Each morning the prisoners gathered up all the energy they could muster. As weeks of marching turned into months, guards abandoned feeble and ailing prisoners along the road or in barns and huts. No one was ever sure what happened to those left behind. One only hoped that they would be shown mercy. Nightmares haunted men who worried about buddies left behind. Guards disappeared as time went on. Desertion was preferable to starvation or capture by the Allies. The guards were not the only ones who thought about escaping.

One night another prisoner approached Pifer. Schmidt, a second-generation German from North Dakota, was looking for single men interested in participating in an escape attempt. When Schmidt first came up with the idea, he found that most of the married men didn't want to take the chance. However, he felt it was worth the risk and wanted to get home to his wife and family. He was fed up with the aimless march.

"Would you be interested?" he asked. And Pifer agreed. Pifer tried to convince his combine partner, Wayne Moeller, to join them, but to no avail. But another bachelor, Kremper, said he was willing to take the chance.

From reports received on the road, they knew that American and English forces were gaining ground in Germany and that the Russians were still pushing westward. The prisoners were sure they could reach the front line of the Allied forces.

Kremper said he had some cans of sardines sewn into the lining of his coat. He had managed to stash them from the Red Cross parcel he received in February. Without a centralized distribution point, the Germans did not get a chance to puncture any of the cans and he had kept his sardines for such an occasion as this. He was willing to share with Schmidt and Pifer while they were in hiding. The three sought out Miller, their group leader, to discuss their plans.

Miller pointed out that the column was marching in a westerly direction. He felt they were headed back to Fallingbostel and Stalag 11B. "As long as we are going west, you are safer with us than you are out there by yourself," he told them. However, realizing that the three had made up their minds to escape, he negotiated with them. "If we start marching east again, then I'll help you tighten up your plans," he promised. They acquiesced.

Without the support of their leader, the prisoners knew their escape could not work. Once men decided to run for it, a leader was necessary to coordinate activities to hide their disappearance during roll calls. By remaining on the road a while longer, it would be easier to hide their departure because the longer they marched the more disorganized the guards became. Not altogether happy with the idea of waiting, Schmidt, Pifer, and Kremper agreed that Miller was right and obeyed his orders. They would wait for a more opportune time.

Some escapees from camps and marching columns were lucky to find the Allied forces in the spring of 1945, but in most cases, the men who remained in prisoner-of-war camps were the more fortunate. As Allied forces reached Stalags, Oflags, and Stalag Lufts, they liberated the camps. It took longer for the American and British troops to find columns of marching prisoners that zigzagged out of their reach.

Trees heavy with buds now leafed out. Small green shoots began to peek through the rich dark soil of the German countryside. Prisoners began to shed layers of clothes. Pifer traded his jacket to a peasant for some bread and cheese. Desertion among the ranks of guards steadily rose as the column moved east again. Rumors of Allied progress kept Schmidt, Kremper, and Pifer marching in the column, instead of initiating their escape plan.

The column crisscrossed northern Germany into small villages and towns like Blackede, Geese, Erfurt, and Büchen. In Lüneburg on the Ilmenau River, they saw buildings that dated from the thirteenth century and wondered if the structures would survive the increased bombings of the final offensive. Medieval churches, cathedrals, and castles rose out of the forests or stood proudly on hilltops.

In Erfurt, the Augustinian monastery where Martin Luther was ordained in 1507 stood in stark contrast to bombed commercial areas. A twelfth-century tradesman bridge, which was lined with shops, crossed a canal. They marched through the heart of Germany's agricultural centers, past huge feudal estates once owned by Prussian aristocratic elite. The prisoners and their guards traversed river valleys and crossed mighty bodies of water.

After getting off one ferry, they saw it blown out of the water by a British fighter swooping out of the sky. The prisoners found shelter in the forests of oak, ash, elm, beech, birch, and pine. From the marshes of the northern coast to the flat rolling hills that rose to meet the southern mountains, the German guards and their prisoners had been evading the Allied and Russians troops for eighty-seven days.

They had marched north past the city of Wittenberge in east-central Germany. The city was a railroad junction and manufacturing center, but was particularly well known for its role in the Protestant Reformation. In 1517, Martin Luther nailed his ninety-five theses to the door of the Castle Church. They had been following the Elbe-Lübeck Canal for several days when the guards led their column of prisoners to a large farm near Wittenberge.

Weary men made beds in the farmhouse and in the hayloft and stalls of the two-story barn. On the night of May 1st, the last of the men to arrive fell asleep not knowing what the next day would bring.

CHAPTER SEVENTEEN

LIBERATION

There was a slight chill in the morning air as the American prisoners assembled outside the barn in the early hours of May 2, 1945. The men milled around the farmyard, stretching tired muscles and readying their possessions for the march. Their bodies no longer filled out their uniforms. Empty stomachs appeared distended on scarecrow frames. Even though the men drew near to the Elbe's swollen banks, they were not allowed to stop and bathe. Their long hair hung filthy and stringy, filled with vermin. The prisoners had not had a shower, haircut, or good shave since they left Stalag 11B. Resigned to another day of marching, they fell into formation.

The American airmen at the front of the column heard the sound of motors coming down the lane leading to the farmyard. When they realized that the vehicles were not German, but were British jeeps and lorries, they stood with open mouths. "What's happening?" someone asked.

The German guards moved toward the British unit with their guns pointed to the ground. The news of the arrival of British soldiers rippled through the rest of the column. They gathered close to hear what the officer had to say. After praying for so many months for the Allied forces to find them, the men believed

Liberation! Unidentified group of American ex-prisoners of war at
their liberation on May 2, 1945. Courtesy of Donald Kremper.

the familiar jeeps and uniforms were an apparition, or German
disguised as British.

A captain stood up in the lead jeep and announced, "You are
officially liberated!"

It took the prisoners of war a few seconds to comprehend
what the young Brit had said. The young flyers, now ex-prisoners of war, turned to each other in disbelief and hope. Were they
really free? The war was over? They were overwhelmed after the
constant marching, cruel treatment, and starvation, so the words
took awhile to sink in.

Then hysterical screams and cheers erupted. Tears welled up
and spilled over. Some of the German guards threw down their
guns. Others reluctantly gave up their arms when confronted
by angry prisoners. Guards and prisoners alike turned to each
other, hugging, laughing, and crying. Pifer hugged Moeller and
they jumped up and down until they fell in a heap. They sprang

to their feet and hugged as many of their buddies as they could grab. Everywhere men were hugging and jumping up and down. Someone had a flag and waved it back and forth. Free at last! Freedom, it was such a beautiful word. Others dropped to their knees to thank God.

It was a while before the British captain could speak. The noise of the celebrating flyers filled the farmyard and spilled into the woods around them. Eventually, the grinning, shouting, and crying men quieted down. Word spread through the crowd that the captain and his unit were an outfit under the leadership of Field Marshal Montgomery. Since the area was not secured yet, the captain advised the American ex-prisoners of war and their German guards to continue marching toward Büchen approximately fifteen to twenty miles away. With the Germans in their ranks, the column would be safe if any SS troops were encountered. The captain told the group that the front line of the Allied forces was just to the southwest of them. He would send trucks to meet them in Büchen.

The black period of marching aimlessly around Germany had come to an end after eighty-seven days and over six hundred miles. Men, who had kept a log of the march, now jubilantly wrote the word "liberated" in their books. The column continued to follow the road south and west towards the village of Büchen. Every once in awhile, an airman moved to take a guard's gun.

To reassure himself that he was truly free, Pifer walked for some distance with one of the German guards and they talked brokenly, not as captor and captive, but as two men marching toward freedom. The guard was ready and willing to end the war as a prisoner of the British. He was tired of the fighting and welcomed an end to the aimless marching. The weight of the gun in Pifer's hand felt good, and he realized he didn't even mind the final hike toward freedom.

German leader surrendering to the commander of the English Sixth Airborne, May 2, 1945. The men in the background are American prisoners of war whom German guards were marching all over Germany in what has been called the Black March. Courtesy of Donald Kremper.

As the sun set, the marchers began looking for a place to stay the night. They finally found an abandoned farm near Gudow. The men filled the house, barn, and sheds. Ex-prisoners ran into the farmhouse to enjoy the normalcy of being in a real home with actual beds and furniture to sit on. Men took turns jumping on the mattresses, sitting on overstuffed furniture, and eating whatever they could find in the larder. Eventually, they settled in for the night and a contingent of men traded off, keeping watch over the sleeping prisoners and remaining German guards.

On the morning of May 3rd, Pifer and another prisoner awoke and left the shelter of the barn. As they stood in the farmyard talking about their homes in Pennsylvania, Pifer and Estep were startled by the arrival of a communications truck. A German officer and sergeant sprang out of the truck with their hands in the air. Looking at each other, Pifer and Estep realized at that moment the war had come full circle and they laughed heartily. Pifer turned to the German soldiers and smugly said, "For *you*, the war is over."

The two giddy Army Air Corps sergeants ran toward the truck and its trailer. They madly threw things out of the cab of the truck. Estep jumped in behind the steering wheel and Pifer swung around to the passenger side. The hooting and hollering of the two awakened others. Rubbing the sleep from their eyes, they saw the truck and trailer in the yard and ran toward it. Men piled onto the hood, the trailer, the back of the truck—anywhere they could get a hold. The noise from so many laughing and shouting brought out even more men.

Pifer yelled at Estep to drive the hell out of there, *now*, before the truck was so full it wouldn't move. Heading toward the Elbe River, they figured they would find the British and American front line. The men in the truck and trailer were following the road on the east side of the river when they met an English scout car with twin .50-calibers mounted on it. The Brits stopped the truck and shouted, "Wherever you are going, turn this thing around and head back, because there's a bunch of SS troops ahead!"

Estep and Pifer looked at each other and decided they did not want to tackle the SS any more than the Brits in their scout car did. Estep reached for the stick shift and tried to put the truck in reverse and it lunged forward, jerking its occupants back and forth. He did not realize that in German vehicles the gearshift had to be pushed down, then over, to engage reverse.

Several of the others in the cab frantically tried to find reverse. Pifer suggested that they unhitch the trailer, then push the truck around. Men piled out of the truck and pushed as Estep steered.

Finally, the truck was headed in the right direction. Others hitched the trailer back to the truck and then scrambled aboard. The truck and trailer overflowing with men headed back to the farm they had left. They had to get there as quickly as possible and warn the rest of the column about the advancing SS troop.

The truck roared into the empty farmyard. One of the men ran into the barn and another toward the farmhouse. "No one is here!" they yelled.

Unbeknownst to the errant group, British trucks had arrived to carry the main column to a safe haven. They had already crossed the canal at Büchen and were headed to a pontoon bridge on the Elbe River. Guessing where to go, Estep spun the truck around in a wide circle and headed to the village of Büchen. The villagers rushed out with shotguns or whatever weapon they could find. One of the Americans pulled off his dirty, once white, underwear and hitched it on the end of a rifle. With a flag of truce waving in the air, the truck with its laughing and shouting passengers barreled down the road.

They followed the road to Lüneburg and down to the banks of the Elbe River. There the joy riders caught up with the rest of their column. On the afternoon of May 3, 1945, the ex-prisoners of Stalag Luft 4 crossed a pontoon bridge on the Elbe and entered the Allied secured area of western Europe.

A large group of British soldiers welcomed the Army Air Corps flyers in Lüneburg, where a temporary camp had been established. British medical staff deloused the vermin-infested airmen. Kremper hacked away at Pifer's straggly hair with a pair of scissors he had found in the German communications truck. With shorn head and face and clean clothes, Pifer felt like a soldier again.

Doctors cautioned the emaciated men to begin to eat slowly and in small amounts to alleviate intestinal problems. Many of the men, starved for so long, found it difficult to restrain themselves. It wasn't long after a meal that they sprinted to the latrines.

On May 4th, on Lüneburg Heath, the commander-in-chief of the Allied 21st Army Group, Field Marshal Montgomery, met with a German delegation headed by Admiral Hans von Friede-burg to accept the surrender of the German forces in north-western Germany, Holland, and Denmark. However, to the east, fierce fighting continued.

The American airmen celebrated with Montgomery's men in their makeshift camp. On the morning of May 7th, a British soldier directed Pifer and the rest of the freed prisoners to trucks that would take them to an airfield near Lüneburg. On the runway, a C-47 transport carrier waited to fly them to Brussels, Belgium.

Pifer crammed into the wide-bodied plane with his buddies and listened to the comforting purr of the mighty engines. The airmen were glad, so glad, to be back aboard a flying machine. A cheer went up as the plane shuddered and lifted off. Even though Germany was the homeland of his grandfather and his ancestors, Pifer never wanted to set foot on German soil again. He was an American through and through.

That same day, the Germans surrendered unconditionally to American General Dwight Eisenhower at his headquarters in Reims, France. The war in Europe was over.

CHAPTER EIGHTEEN

CIGARETTE CAMPS

Field Marshal Montgomery's men transported the liberated prisoners of war to reception camps in France and Belgium. Traveling via planes, trucks, and trains, the men arrived at various Allied camps. Upon arrival in camp, the prisoner of war became a RAMP—a Repatriated Allied Military Person.

After landing in Brussels, Pifer and his buddies climbed aboard trucks that took them to a British reception center. In an open area near a sea of tents, the airmen saw a stand of crosses in a single row. On each white cross, the name of a country was printed. A soldier directed the men to line up behind the cross that identified the country they served.

Pifer followed a group of men to the cross bearing the initials U.S. Since their liberation, these young men couldn't stop grinning. Their elation had not ebbed but only grew as they began the processing that would carry them home again. It was really happening! It was not a dream. They were back with the U.S. Army.

As the lines grew behind the crosses, a soldier led small groups away to medical tents identified by large lettered signs tacked near the doorways and a large red cross on the side. While trucks continued to unload men, Canadians, British, Finns, Americans, and others lined up behind a cross. There were so many men to

Dispensary Area at an unidentified cigarette camp. Author's collection.

be processed, it took quite a while to get through the lines, but everyone waiting patiently, laughing and talking. Finally, Pifer was led away with a group of fifteen to twenty airmen.

At a table near the front of the tent, a medic asked, "Do you have any problems with dysentery? Any unusual coughing or lingering shortness of breath?" Once Pifer answered all the medic's questions, he moved through the line to have blood drawn and get tested for tuberculosis. He was encouraged to drink lots and lots of eggnog for protein. His shrunken stomach would expand as he increased his food intake, but it was important to do this slowly to avoid gastrointestinal problems. Doctors examined him for any residual effects caused by the months of malnutrition in the prisoner-of-war camps and on the march. A medic gave the young flyer a typhus shot and sent him on his way.

From the medical tent, Pifer was led to a supply tent, where he was handed a set of clothes and a new pair of shoes. He hungrily ran his hand over the fabric and the rough leather of his new shoes. Having lived fourteen months in the same set of clothes, he relished the thought of getting into his new duds. After being deloused a second time, Pifer changed into them. His old clothes were thrown in one pile to be burned and his boots in another. The supply clerks were astounded that so many of the Americans had literally worn out their army boots. Patches had been put on patches. There were so many patches on the soles and leather uppers that, for most wearers, little of the original boot remained. Never before had the clerks seen completely worn out army boots.

At the processing tent, Pifer sent his first cablegram to his family, telling them that he was safe and sound. The preprinted form had a series of boxes lined up neatly behind pretyped sentences that stated he was in British/United States hands, was well and safe, would write as soon as possible, and expected to be home soon. One section provided information to families about their sons and husbands who were hospitalized. Next to the line "Expect to be home soon," Larry penciled a large check that almost spilled out of the box. He signed his name with a flourish and dated the telegram.

From the message center, he moved to a cash line. An Army clerk counted out 840 French francs into the young man's hand. The Brit told him he was free to go anywhere he wanted to, but if he wanted to rejoin the rest of the Americans, he was to report to the train station by seven o'clock that the evening.

Small clusters of American flyers left the installation and headed to town. The infantrymen at the front gate told them if they needed anything, anything at all, just let them know, they would take good care of them. The American airmen felt like kings with money in their pockets and their newfound freedom to roam wherever they wanted to go. They headed to town.

EX PRISONER OF WAR
FIELD POST CARD

FOR ADDRESS ONLY

The address only to be written on this side.

If anything else is added, the card will be destroyed.

TO

Miss Helen Pifer

1331 Linwood Ave.

Niagra Falls, N.Y.

U.S.A.

NOTHING is to be written on this side except the date and signature of the sender. If anything else is added the postcard will be destroyed.

Mark the sentences or phrases below thus ✓

I am in British / U. S. hands ✓

I am well and safe ✓

Will write as soon as possible ✓

Expect to be home soon ✓
    Do not write

I have been admitted to hospital.
        sick.   Am going on well
        wounded.   Hope to be discharged soon

Signature _Lawrence D. Pifer_

Date _MAY -4-1945_

Received May 19, 45.

SA/PSS/4.

Ex-POW field postcard. Postcard that T/Sgt. Lawrence Pifer mailed from Field Post 295 on May 7, 1945, to his sister Helen. Courtesy of Lawrence Pifer.

At a small shop off a square, Larry bought a wallet to stow his money. Most of the airmen went in search of food and drink. Men in uniform spilled out of cafes and bars onto the narrow brick and cobbled streets of Brussels' commercial districts. Small groups wandered the streets looking for bookstores or just taking in the sights, including the girls. Fathers kept their daughters close and hollered at many admirers to move on.

For over four years the Germans had occupied Brussels, the industrial and rail center of Belgium. In May of 1945, Brussels was in the midst of a building boom to replace the bombed-out sections of the city. In September, the government returned from Britain and, with the Allied forces' protection, devoted all its energy to rebuilding the country's financial and commercial infrastructure. The Gothic buildings surrounding the "Grand Place" in the center of Brussels had withstood the German bombardment and invasion.

Four- and five-story stone buildings crowded the narrow, winding streets leading away from a central square. Fanciful and lavish decorative ornamentation on the face of the buildings identified the stonework of various master craftsmen. Over the door of one particularly plain stone building an ornamental goose, standing below a fanciful arbor, spread her wings, breaking free from the bondage of the stone just as the American airmen had broken free from their German shackles.

Long before their seven o'clock deadline, men crowded the platform of the main rail station, watching for the arrival of the train. No one wanted to miss the train to Namur, Belgium, where the American forces were located. Many of the flyers and soldiers just wanted to put as much distance between Germany and themselves as quickly as possible. Pifer and his friends clambered aboard a rail car and found seats near the middle of the car.

They were traveling in style now—real seats. As the train left Brussels behind and picked up speed, a vendor traveled up and down the aisles selling sandwiches, snacks, and drinks. The ex-prisoners ate, talked, sang songs, and watched the scenery fly by. Before the travelers realized it, their trip was over. At the end of the line, the Americans had set up a staging area and a committee greeted the new arrivals.

The ex-prisoners arriving at the station were told not to pass the painted line on the road into Namur. Military personnel guarded that checkpoint. The town was strictly off-limits to army personnel. This order was the first indication that they were back in the army.

While they were with the British, no one ordered them about and they were allowed to roam at will. Pifer and his buddies speculated whether they should have stayed in Brussels with their British hosts. For now, the men milled around until trucks came to carry them off to the deployment camp, Camp Twenty Grand, near the village of Duclair, France.

Until their embarkation camp was ready, the men would spend a day or two in Camp Twenty Grand. The city of tents and temporary buildings had hospitals, kitchens, and American Red Cross "Java Junction" tents offering coffee and doughnuts. Being in an American camp infused them with a new energy. Plentiful and hot food was the biggest draw.They couldn't complain about the entertainment, either. A makeshift theater set up under the stars provided movies. That night Pifer got to see his first movie since leaving England in March of 1944.

As the shadows fell, the men found seats on wooden benches in front of the screen. A wind began to pick up, but they ignored it as the light of the projector flickered and the Parisian-born movie star, Claudette Colbert, appeared on the screen. The moviegoers whistled and cheered at the sight of the brunette beauty. Within minutes, a drizzle began and soon rain fell, but the film operator covered the projector with a tarp and the old movie continued. The men remained in their seats. They had marched and

Unidentified cigarette camp in France. Author's collection.

slept in the rain as prisoners and it did not faze them now. Watching Claudette was well worth sitting through a little rain.

Camp Lucky Strike near Le Havre, France, was ready to accept the RAMPs. Once again, the ex-prisoners climbed aboard green Army transport trucks to travel to their next destination.

The airfield at Lucky Strike had been built in 1939. The French erected a wartime aerodrome on a point overlooking the *Baie de la Seine* where the Seine River empties into the English Channel. When the Germans captured the aerodrome, they constructed a large concrete runway from which to send their bombers out over England. Lighting was added for night reconnaissance. The engineers positioned the runways in a circle, allowing space for the farms and castles around the airfield. When the Germans pulled out in September 1944, they detonated bombs to destroy the runways, but in a short time the Allied engineers had them repaired and functioning. The aerodrome then became Camp Lucky Strike, a transit camp and deployment center for arriving troops. It was turned into a village of canvas tents with over 100,000 United States soldiers staying overnight at any given time.

As the war drew to a close in Europe in May 1945, the countryside was washed in green. Fields released their humus smells, masking the stench of death and war. As the warm winds blew across the coastal region of France, they tugged at the tent flaps in Camp Lucky Strike. The airmen were about thirty-five miles from the port of Le Havre. In the rolling fields near the coast, the repatriated gathered to await transport home to the United States.

At this, their final embarkation point, the ex-prisoners wrote lengthier cables, explaining to their families where they were and what they were doing. Pifer sent cables to his father, sister, and aunt, telling them that he would be home as soon as possible. He sent his aunt, who had been like a mother to him all these years, a belated Mother's Day greeting.

At home in Clearfield, Pennsylvania, the local paper ran a piece telling everyone that Ivan Pifer had received a telegram from his son, who had been liberated from a German prison camp.

Upon arrival at the embarkation center, Pifer and his buddies met with doctors, supply clerks, and camp officials. Camp doctors reiterated the importance of rest and proper nourishment for the ex-prisoners' severely taxed bodies. Their diet at Camp Lucky Strike included a lot of canned turkey and Spam, a ham product. At first, despite doctor's warnings, many of the men gorged themselves and in consequence suffered numerous stomach ailments. The ex-prisoners could not shake the fear that the food would disappear. The long chow lines served to improve their hunger.

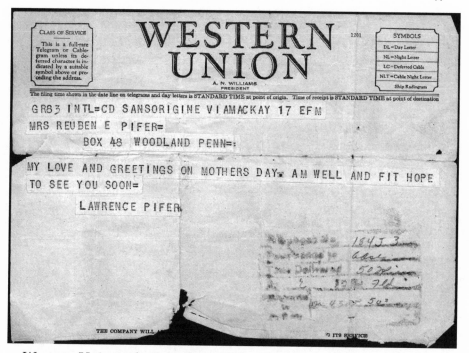

Western Union telegram from T/Sgt. Lawrence Pifer to his aunt, Helen Pifer. Helen carried it with her and read it so many times that it became worn where she folded it. Courtesy of Lawrence Pifer.

Slowly the men gained back the weight they had lost in captivity. During his incarceration, Pifer dropped seventy-five pounds, weighing in at only ninety pounds when he was liberated. Within a month, he had almost returned to his normal weight.

Embarkation camps were often reunion scenes. Separated from their airships, their units, even their prison camp buddies, men found each other through lists posted on camp bulletin boards. Even so, in a community of approximately 100,000 men, it was hard to find anyone. At Camp Lucky Strike, Pifer was reunited with his combine buddy, Wayne Moeller, and the remaining *Slightly Dangerous II* crew.

During the airlifts to Brussels, Pifer had gotten separated from Moeller and had not been able to find him again. He was devastated. A special bond developed between prisoners sharing their ordeal in the prisoner-of-war camps and on their forced marches. Dividing their food and blankets, even nursing each other when ill, combine buddies exchanged far more of themselves than material goods. They shared trust and respect. Searching as much as he was able, Larry had not found Moeller in the sea of tents in the camp. Then, purely by accident, the two men ran into each other.

Walking through the rows of tents one day, Pifer passed an airman who looked familiar to him. He paused, turned around, and saw that the other airman was also looking back. They both shook their heads and continued on their way. When he arrived at the day tent, a place to meet others and play cards and games, he spied Clyde Forrester, who had been a radio operator on Wayne Moeller's bomber crew. "Hey Forrester, have you seen Moeller since you got here?" Puzzled, Clyde replied, "You must have just passed him!"

Larry turned and hurried back the way he came. He and Wayne laughed over the fact that they did not recognize each other since they had gained so much weight. They explained what had happened to them since boarding the transport plane in Brussels and promised to keep in touch.

Reading the lists posted on the bulletin board, Pifer learned that the remaining crew of *Slightly Dangerous II* was also at Camp Lucky Strike. He found their tents and they caught up on what had been going on in their lives since that pivotal day in March 1944. That eighteenth mission finally had come to an end off the coast of France over a year later, in May of 1945. Many comrades had been lost. Now they were ready to go home.

With the end of the war in Europe, the transit camps once set up as deployment centers were now busily engaged in redirecting troops and ex-prisoners. Reinforcement troops moved into police-occupied territories. Others were diverted to the Pacific Theater. Many hoped to be redeployed to the United States. Troop movement was of immediate importance. The former prisoners waited patiently in Camp Lucky Strike for a transport home.

They spent a great deal of time sleeping, eating, playing cards, and writing letters. Small groups of men talked about their families. Others walked along the coast of France and gazed out upon the ocean, watching and waiting. Pifer found he had more trouble adjusting to freedom than he had to being taken prisoner. Many of the others felt the same way. His time at Camp Lucky Strike was like a dream. Surrounded by thousands of men, he felt it was the sort of life he had led as a POW, only cleaner and with better food. Pifer found it hard to imagine he was truly free.

Immediately after the end of the war in Europe, government and military officials flew in to evaluate the damages. Ships from around the world were dispatched to carry troops home. Specially assigned naval vessels called "Liberty" ships transported the American armed forces to port cities such as Norfolk, Baltimore, and New York City. Forty-eight thousand men were processed and debriefed in Camp Lucky Strike during the month of May. At the end of the month, Pifer was waiting for his transport when General Eisenhower arrived to speak to the men.

Shaking hands with as many as possible, Eisenhower walked down the chow line and wished them all well. It was a thrill for Pifer and the rest of the airmen to meet and shake hands with the revered general. Addressing the group, the general explained he wanted them to have first-class accommodations back to the States. However, because there were so many ex-prisoners, the ship entering the port at Le Havre could not accommodate all of them.

T/Sgt. Lawrence Pifer's embarkation card. Each serviceman was required to have embarkation cards before boarding ships to leave Europe. Courtesy of Lawrence Pifer.

Eisenhower gave the men a choice of traveling in first class with a limited load of passengers on the ship, which meant leaving some behind to wait for another ship, or double-loading the ship. Double-loading meant that each man would have to share a bunk and alternate days of sleep. The first twenty-four hours they would have a bunk, and none during the next. The eager men had been waiting almost a month to get a ride home to the United States, and no one wanted to be left behind. They voted to double-up.

Strains of Old Glory danced on the air as streams of men climbed the gangway to the Liberty ship, *Marine Robin*, on June 2, 1945. Clutching embarkation papers in one hand and a sleeping bag in the other, each man presented his card to a naval clerk before climbing aboard the ship.

Pifer shifted his duffle bag and moved forward in the line. Cocked at an angle, his hat gave him a cavalier look. The line of men in new uniforms and spotlessly polished boots snaked its way down the pier toward the transport home.

After days of languishing in the cigarette camps, the alacrity of their final processing and departure from Le Havre left Pifer in a state of shock. For months, he had prayed for freedom and a chance to get home to his family. The safety net of military routine and day-to-day activities in Camp Lucky Strike were gone. Altered by his experience, he was, like many of the men, apprehensive about returning to the old life at home. Finally, the ramp loomed in front of him. The naval clerk checked Pifer's papers and welcomed the airman aboard.

Seamen went to work readying the ship for departure. The airmen and soldiers crowded close to the railing of the ship. As the coast of France slowly disappeared, they were torn between a desire to remain in France and their need to go home. Waves of emotions buffeted the men standing at the railing watching the French coastline shrink away. After months of controlling their emotions in prisoner-of-war camps, the realization that they were truly heading home to the United States unleashed pent-up emotions and tears flowed down their cheeks. Cheers went up. Others turned away and withdrew into themselves. All were irrevocably changed. They would never be the nineteen- and twenty-year-olds that eagerly and patriotically signed up to serve their country in its moment of crisis. Those enthusiastic and naive men filled with patriotism and dreams of romantic adventure were forever dead. Their souls were scarred, crushed, even destroyed, by the horrors of war. Could or would their families recognize the men they had become?

When the men could no longer see land, they turned away from the rail. It was time to explore the ship; it would be their home for the next week. The ship's crew assigned bunks to the ex-prisoners and explained the bunk rotation. Wandering the ship's deck on his first twenty-four hours without a bunk, Pifer spied a ledge near some electrical motors. A ladder led up to it.

Glancing left and right to see if anyone was around, Pifer mounted the ladder. He decided that the space was large enough to unroll his sleeping bag. High above the activity of the ship, he felt almost alone. Every inch of the ship was filled with navy and army personnel and this was one spot that was not. After months of being hemmed in from all sides by barbed wire fences or being shackled to men, he decided he would rather share his space with a machine than with a man. When his bunkmate came looking for him the next day to trade out, Pifer told him to keep the bunk because he had found his own spot and was quite comfortable.

During the day, small groups of men played cards or board games. Others walked the decks, watching the sea and its creatures. Everyone got excited and ran to the railing when whales were sighted off the bow of the ship. Occasionally, a seaman would shoot off a couple rounds near the whales. The *Marine Robin* was completely alone in a watery universe. There were no escort ships. Days passed before they finally saw land.

The *Marine Robin* sailed into New York Harbor on June 8, 1945. Shouts and cheers broke out when the coast of New York was sighted. Like the immigrants who had entered the harbor over the decades, the returning airmen and soldiers were overcome with joy at seeing the Statue of Liberty. Some cheered and others cried as the ship churned past the green lady holding her torch.

The *Marine Robin* anchored and was placed in quarantine before the men were allowed to disembark. It was painful to be so close to home and not be able to set foot on United States soil. Finally, the port authorities allowed the ship to make its way up the Hudson River and down the East River to dock in the deep waters east of Manhattan. The arriving airmen were escorted to the train station to catch a train to Camp Shanks, New York. The Red Cross canteen at the station served coffee and doughnuts to the men while they waited for the next train to arrive.

At Camp Shanks, the men were issued new uniforms and gear. Then it was off to Camp Kilmer, New Jersey, for debriefing and processing. The next few days were a blur for Pifer. Before he knew it, a clerk at Camp Kilmer was handing him a furlough pass and a partial paycheck. The stipend was enough to purchase a ticket home. The clerk told Pifer that he would get his back pay when he returned from leave.

Because the war waged on in the Pacific, none of the men were discharged. The clerk told Pifer to meet his group in Miami Beach, Florida, on August 16th where he would be reassigned a duty station in the Pacific. Before he realized it, Larry Pifer was on a train headed to Pennsylvania.

CHAPTER NINETEEN

GOING HOME

After changing trains a couple of times, Larry took one to Tyrone, Pennsylvania, the nearest station to Clearfield. His father had moved from Sykesville to Clearfield just before he had gone in the army. Larry didn't know his father's phone number, so he was on his own in getting to his father's house. From Tyrone, he would have to find a lift to Clearfield, about thirty-six miles away.

When the train pulled into the station, it was past midnight. Golden pools of light from the street lamps ringed the dark, empty streets. No light spilled from the windows of the buildings lining the sidewalks; even the hotels were dark. On the platform, a small knot of people waited expectantly for family and friends. Larry paused on the bottom step of the car and watched as friends and family greeted each other with hugs and kisses. Small groups drifted away into the night until eventually he was the only one left standing on the platform. The station attendant spying Larry's army uniform came up and told him that there was a canteen inside the station.

Fred Waring and his band, a popular dance band originating from the Tyrone and Altoona area, funded canteens in local rail stations to supply refreshment for traveling servicemen. A band of volunteers worked the canteen twenty-four hours a day handing out coffee and doughnuts and welcoming each serviceman. While Larry ate his pastry, he watched the street for any signs of traffic and not one car or truck had passed the station. Feeling sure that it would be easier to hitch a ride home in the morning, he decided to spend the night in the station. He considered the benches in the waiting area and chose one near the back of the room and out of the line of the door. After the sleeping conditions he had endured in German prison camps, he thought the bench looked mighty comfortable. Using his duffel bag for a pillow, Larry settled in for a brief nap.

A few hours later, a policeman sauntered in and stopped by the canteen for a cup of coffee and visit with the volunteer. She pointed in Larry's direction. Awakened by the slamming of the station door, Larry watched as the policeman walked toward him. "Now what," he thought to himself. Maybe he wouldn't be able to stay in the rail station after all.

The policeman asked, "Are you the one looking for a ride to Clearfield?" When Larry nodded, he told him to wait. The policeman turned and headed out the door and down the street towards the nearest intersection. After stopping a variety of vehicles, he found a tractor-trailer truck going to Curwensville, about ten miles beyond Clearfield. The trucker readily agreed to give the young airman a lift. "Anything for a man in uniform!" he told the policeman, who hurried back to fetch Larry. Carrying his duffel bag, Larry climbed into the truck cab. Finally he was on the last leg of his journey home. Home. The thought made his stomach lurch.

The lights of the truck illuminated the winding tree-lined road. The words from the poem, "Over the river and through the woods," ran through Larry's head as the trees skimmed by. The sun rising over the Pennsylvania hills nudged wisps of fog out of low-lying areas. Lights glowed in houses along the roadway.

It was about six in the morning when the truck lumbered down Brewery Hill into Clearfield. The driver stopped his truck on Railroad Street near the corner of Nichols Street, where Larry's father now lived. Larry thanked the trucker again for the lift and he hopped out onto the sidewalk.

As he turned away from the main commercial district and walked into the neighborhood, Larry could see lights on in the kitchens of the houses he passed. Inside their homes, families were eating their breakfast or getting ready for work. After the interruption of war, he found comfort in, even marveled at, the continuance of normal everyday life at home.

Larry made his way up the familiar tree-lined street. When he left for the service, his father was living on Walnut Street in Clearfield, but Helen told him that their father had moved to Nichols Street. Larry had the address written on a slip of paper in his pocket and pulled it out to check the street number again.

Larry hurried up the front steps of the porch and saw that a window was open. Wouldn't his father be surprised? Instead, Larry was surprised to find a stranger, who had no idea of his father's whereabouts. After borrowing the woman's phone to call his Uncle Reuben for a ride, Larry settled on the top step of the porch to wait. It was not the homecoming he expected, but surely his uncle would know where to look for his father.

While Larry waited on the steps, the new tenant remembered that a woman named Violet had previously lived at the house. She phoned her with the story about the young airman arriving home from the war. Violet, who was still living with Ivan, called him at work. Ivan immediately got permission to leave work for the day.

Waiting in the morning sun, Larry dozed. He had gotten very little sleep, except for catnaps, since leaving the liberty ship in New York. Trying to stay awake, he thought about all the things that had happened to him since he left home and Clearfield so many months and years ago.

When Larry left Pennsylvania after graduating from high school, he was only seventeen and looking for an adventure. He never imagined his travels would eventually lead him to enlist in the Army Air Corps or that he would end up halfway around the world in a prisoner-of-war camp in Germany. He had left home in 1940 and enlisted in 1942. Now it was June of 1945. No one had expected the war to last very long, but everyone had been wrong. Larry felt he had spent half his life in the military and prison camps. Now he was home. Little appeared to have changed in Clearfield. He thought perhaps he *could* walk back into his old life and begin over again.

A car pulled up to the curb in front of the house. Aunt Helen and Uncle Reuben peered out through the windshield expectantly. They must have jumped into their car immediately and headed to town. No sooner had they turned off the car ignition than Larry's father arrived. There was a moment of indecision. Should he go with his aunt and uncle or with his father?

Larry stopped a moment to greet and thank his aunt and uncle for coming. He would ride to his father's house with him, but would be by soon to see them. With Recuperation and Rehabilitation Orders in his pocket, Larry headed off to his father's house on the outskirts of town.

After the war, the United States seemed like a foreign country to many returning servicemen and ex-prisoners. They were overcome by the noise and bustle of the city; even the din of small-town activities became unbearable. Bands and parades met some arriving servicemen, but for the most part, it was a solitary soldier or airman riding or walking home to some small town in America.

When his father asked him what he would like to do, Larry told him he wanted to go a barbershop and get a decent haircut.

It felt heavenly to settle into the leather barber chair. Ivan sat waiting. As the barber began combing and clipping Larry's hair, Ivan told him that Larry had just gotten back from the war after being in Germany for fourteen months. When talk turned to congratulations and the war, Larry squirmed, feeling self-conscious and pinned to the chair like a beetle tacked to a board in a bug collection. Finally, the barber shook out the cape and Larry was free to go. From the barbershop, he and his father went to the office of the War Department to pick up the gasoline coupons promised to each airman and soldier.

When war broke out after the dark days of the Great Depression, inflation caused the prices of consumer goods to rise dramatically. To rein in inflation, the 1940 Anti-Inflation Act allowed the Roosevelt administration to freeze agricultural prices, wages, and rents.[1] Shortages of consumer goods, such as gasoline, rubber, fuel oil, and perishable food items, prompted food and gas rationing. The Office of Price Administration oversaw the program, but state-rationing administrators oversaw the distribution of coupon books. To be equitable, the government distributed ration books of stamps based upon each family's needs. School superintendents and teachers were enlisted to register families in every community. Local rationing boards, made up mostly of volunteers, registered families and distributed information about the program to members of their communities.

After registering, families received ration books through the mail. Every person in the household, including every child, got a ration book for each period. A large poster was placed in every grocer's store. The Official Table of Point Values was the standard for all stores in the nation. Items like coffee, sugar, meat, butter, and canned goods were purchased at stores with a combination of stamps and cash. The stamps were color coded to identify their respective value in points.

When returning airmen arrived at Camp Kilmer, army personnel told them that they were eligible to receive coupons for one gallon of gasoline for each day of their furlough. In addition, after presenting his leave papers to the local War Price and Rationing Board, the soldier's family would receive a coupon for food to cover the period of his leave. Larry had sixty days of furlough.

Just inside the door of the War Board office, a woman sat at her typewriter tapping away and adding sheets to a pile on her desk. Larry explained to her that he was there to pick up his gasoline coupons and ration stamps. She asked for his papers. The only paper that Larry had been given at Camp Kilmer was a copy of the order authorizing sixty days of rest and rehabilitation at home. It also included his orders to report in August to Miami Beach, Florida, for reassignment to the Pacific Theater.

After reading through his papers, the attendant asked for some other type of identification, such as a driver's license or a draft number to connect him with the Army Air Corps. Larry explained he had neither. She denied his request for coupons.

Larry persisted, explaining that he had just returned home from a prisoner-of-war camp and had lost his wallet with all his identification in it in Germany. The only form of Army identification was his army dog tag and R & R orders, but she would not accept them as such. He asked her to speak to her supervisor.

Shaking her head, the clerk walked into her supervisor's office. Her boss concurred, saying that without a driver's license or draft number Larry was definitely not eligible for coupons. The young airman explained, "I enlisted before I was required to register for the Draft Board." He gave an account of his activities over the last three-plus years. The supervisor peered through his glasses at the young man in uniform and told his clerk to issue the coupons.

American towns were proud of the numbers of boys they sent to fight for their country. For returning servicemen, "who had saved the world from a heinous enemy," they threw welcome-home parties. Townspeople back-slapped their brave fighting men and congratulated them on the battles they had won. Many of the young men felt self-conscious and uncomfortable receiving so much adulation. They were glad to be home, but didn't feel that it was really home any longer. They had changed so much. Still, they attended the dinners and parties that were held on their behalf.

A few weeks after Larry got home, the city commissioner and Clearfield businessmen held a dinner to honor their returning soldiers. Three men had served in the army: Ash Woolridge, an Army officer; Espy Spencer, a gunner on a B-17; and Larry Pifer, a radio operator and ball turret gunner on a B-17. The city commissioner, local businessmen, and political representatives gathered to toast them and their accomplishments.

Since it was army regulations that all serviceman be in uniform at all times, the three arrived in fresh-pressed khakis. After being greeted in the lobby of the Dimeling Hotel, they were escorted by businessmen into the dining room where tables were prepared. Waitresses followed with trays of food. It was a feast, and the young men were flattered that such a spread had been prepared for them, especially since rationing was ongoing and many of the commodities were difficult to get.

After dinner, the city commissioner stood up and began a round of toasts. As he listened to the congratulatory speech, Larry felt awkward. He was sure that the dinner was meant for Lieutenant Woolridge and that the other two had been invited as an afterthought. However, the dinner was nice and he appreciated the accolades. The scene was being repeated across the country. But such festivities could not lift the spirits of many troubled soldiers.

T/Sgt. Lawrence Pifer home on leave in Woodland, Pennsylvania, 1945. Courtesy of Lawrence Pifer.

Visions and memories of battles tormented returning soldiers and ex-prisoners of war. Battle and prison experiences,
as well as the deaths of fellow soldiers or of people at their
own hands, had torn out the hearts of young men and left
them old before their time. Mental images haunted their days
and nights.

In their sleep, servicemen saw dead men who lay in pools of rain, mud, and blood. Emaciated prisoners struggling to survive by scrounging food and eating varmints not meant to be eaten by human beings. Tragic memories of another life, another world, flooded their thoughts even when they were fully awake. Few men like Larry were prepared to deal with the haunting memories. They were such that his family would never understand, even if he wanted to describe what he remembered. So soldiers, airmen, and Larry in particular kept quiet about their war and prison experiences.

His orders said rest and rehabilitation. Did the Army really believe that sixty days of furlough would wash away the memories of the past years? Larry wondered. The first few days after Larry arrived home, he and his dad visited relatives and family friends. His father was proud of him and wanted everyone to see the "war hero" before he had to leave again. Everyone clapped the airman on the back or shook his hand and conveyed esteem for all the boys in uniform. His grandparents celebrated his return and the end of the war in Germany. Pictures were taken. Prayers were said for the boys in the Pacific that they too would be returning home soon. The young airman politely thanked all for their offerings of prayers, meals, and toasts—and slipped away as quickly as possible.

The trauma of war had taken its toll on him. Larry realized that his way of thinking and reasoning had drastically changed as a result of his military experiences and the months in prisoner-of-war camps. He grew anxious in crowds. Being in large groups was unbearable for him. Yet he could not even find comfort with his family. He enjoyed being with his extended family and spent a lot of time with them, but was puzzled and hurt that no one asked about his experiences in Britain and Germany, perhaps being afraid to dredge up old memories and wounds that he was trying to forget. Larry couldn't talk to his father, his sister, grandparents, or aunts and uncles. He felt like a misfit.

Being physically touched was excruciating. After so many months crammed in camps or surrounded day in and day out by other prisoners, Larry craved space and silence. He created a shell around himself. It was impossible to concentrate. His furlough was too short for him to find a job, even if he could find one, and the days stretched long and endless in front of him.

When Larry's military pay resumed, he helped his father and Violet to purchase food and necessities and enjoyed going to the tearoom in Woodland for hamburgers. Since Ivan drove his son's car, the only family vehicle, to and from work, Larry had to walk or hitchhike to get into town or to visit his relatives in Sykesville, about thirty miles from Clearfield. It was not hard for the uniformed serviceman to get rides when he hitchhiked. Then, his sister, Helen, took time off from her job in the ammunitions plant in New York and came to visit.

After she left, Larry decided to see if he could track down the members of his first crew. He considered them brothers, like the ones he had never had, and thought perhaps seeing them would help him over the rough times. He recalled the phone number of P. D. Ralston's mother-in-law in Staunton, Virginia, and called to see if she knew where P. D. was. The elderly woman did not recognize Larry's name until he reminded her about his relationship with P. D. and earlier visits to her home. She seemed confused and disoriented, but Larry did learn that her daughter was living with her and was at work. He thought it was worth a trip to Virginia to see her.

Larry found a ride and arrived in the small Virginia town about the time P. D.'s wife quit work. The young woman was very happy to see Larry, but had the difficult task of telling him that P. D. was killed in action in February of 1944. The B-17 on which P. D. was an assistant flight engineer exploded right after take-off from an airbase in England. It was his first mission.

From a hutch in the dining room, she pulled out photograph albums and the two recalled happy times the three of them had had when the men were training in Walla Walla, Washington. Her brother came over to meet Larry and they went off to a local movie house. The family invited Larry to spend the rest of his leave with them, but he said he needed to get back to Pennsylvania. He would not even stay overnight with them and set out around midnight, hitching a ride north again. Despite his sorrow at finding out about his buddy's death, Larry enjoyed visiting with his family.

A few days later, back in Clearfield, Larry ran into an old friend and after a few uncomfortable minutes struggling to find something to talk about they moved on. It disturbed him that they seemed like complete strangers and couldn't carry on a normal conversation. Another day, he bumped into a former coworker who remarked, "Maybe I should have been in a prisoner-of-war camp! You look in pretty good shape." Startled and at a loss for words, Larry said maybe he should have been and walked on. It appeared that no one knew how to talk to the ex-prisoner, and even he did not know how to make small talk anymore.

Memories haunted him. He tried to write a poem, one to end his logbook, to express his feelings, but he couldn't verbalize the torment tearing him apart inside. War raped many young men of all youthful innocence. They were wizened, hardened men who only wanted to return to the days of their youth, but those days could never be retrieved.

Larry found nights the hardest. The nightmares would begin. The summer humidity smothered him in his second-floor bedroom. Afraid to fall asleep because of the nightmares, he mumbled an excuse to his dad about it being too hot to sleep and that he was going out to see a friend. Night after night, he walked the streets and wished he were a child again. Most of the time, ending up at the local ballpark, he climbed up the bleachers to sit, think, and smoke. He reached into his childhood memories and recalled the crack of the bat and the cheers of the crowd as he rounded third, heading for home. "Will I ever truly feel at home again?" he asked no one in particular.

He rambled through the neighborhoods until he thought he was so tired that he could not possibly dream that night. He was wrong, always wrong. With sleep came the nightmares of being shot down, bombs falling from the sky, and burning alive in a gasoline fire. He could not escape himself or the inner turmoil of his soul.

Over the course of July and August, American ships unmercifully bombarded the islands of Japan. The unstoppable energy with which the Japanese had waged war with the rest of the world was beginning to flag. On August 6, 1945, an American B-29, *Enola Gay*, dropped an atomic bomb on Hiroshima. When a second bomb fell on Nagasaki three days later, the emperor of Japan relented. The war virtually ended in the Far East with the introduction of the atomic holocaust. The army sent a letter to Pifer extending his furlough an additional fifteen days. On September 2, officials of the Japanese government surrendered aboard the battleship *Missouri*.

A trip back to the Clearfield War Department Office for gasoline coupons proved futile. Without a draft number for identification, the clerk did not believe that Larry was an army sergeant. He just looked too young to have enlisted before the draft was instituted and to have served the time in the Army Air Corps that he claimed. In frustration, the young serviceman left the office. He was sure that the clerk thought he was impersonating an enlisted man just to get gasoline coupons. He never went back to prove her wrong.

When Larry's uncle, Luther, heard about his difficulties getting gas coupons, he offered Larry some of his. Farmers received unlimited gasoline coupons because the government considered that they contributed food to the war effort. Luther had more than he needed, he assured his nephew. The extra coupons kept Larry going until he found a gas station in Clearfield whose owner agreed to sell him gas—coupons or not.

As time drew closer to Larry's departure for Florida, Aunt Helen and Violet, talked to him about getting out of the service. They thought Larry had given enough of himself to the army and his country should return home to Pennsylvania to resume a normal life. At first, he stubbornly resisted their advice, but then realized that in many ways he had enjoyed his freedom over the past weeks. There was no one telling him what to do day in and day out. However, he hoped that the regimentation of army life might help him to cope with civilian life. The day-to-day activities would keep him too busy to dwell on the last year of his life. By the time he left Pennsylvania for Florida, he had celebrated his twenty-third birthday. Larry decided it was time to get out of the service—if he could.

When Pifer reported to the hotel where the soldiers were to meet in Miami Beach, Florida, he learned the American government considered the war over with Japan's imminent surrender. The reporting airmen were flown from Florida to San Antonio, Texas, to be awarded honorable discharges. Reading through his discharge papers, Pifer noted that he did not get the automatic promotion that he deserved for being a prisoner of war for over a year. He asked the commander about it. The processing officer told him that if he wanted to reenlist, he could have the promotion immediately. If he didn't reenlist, he would have to stick around a few days and wait for the orders to be processed again. Larry decided not to wait. He declared it was time to return to civilian life.

The Army Air Corps honorably discharged Technical Sgt. Lawrence Pifer on October 5, 1945. The Corps gave each discharged man travel money to return home. Larry took a train from San Antonio to Chicago and from there to Pittsburgh. In Pittsburgh, he transferred to a train headed to Tyrone. Instead of hitching from Tyrone, this time he caught a bus home to Clearfield. When he hopped off the bus near the Kurtz farm, he realized that he was no longer a sergeant in the army. He was a civilian once again. "What in the world will I do for a job?"

He had his back pay to keep him going for a while, but that would soon run out. The first thing was to find transportation. Larry gave his father his old car and went to look for a new one. During the war, car manufacturers had turned to producing war goods. It would take time to reconfigure the plants and return to prewar production. Months would pass before any new cars came off the line.

Perusing for-sale ads in the newspaper, Larry had no luck. The local used-car lots had nothing. Thinking he might have a better chance of finding a car in a larger place, he and a friend, Woody Lansberry, struck out for Meadeville, Pennsylvania.

Finding no likely prospects there, the two stuck out their thumbs once again. The driver of a pickup stopped. He was headed north to Corry, and they gladly jumped at the ride. From Corry, they could go on to nearby Erie.

Woody crawled in the middle and Larry hugged the door of the truck. When Larry learned that the driver was from Corry, he asked, "Do you know a Clarence Barstow?" He did indeed. Clarence had been the driver's best friend before he had gone off to war. He paused a moment and then said that Clarence was missing in action. Clarence's poor mother was still waiting for him to come home from the war. Larry turned to the man and said, "You can tell her he's not coming home. He was killed in action."

The driver shrugged his shoulders and said, "I could never tell Mrs. Barstow that her son was killed unless I was very sure that it was the truth." Only an eyewitness account would convince him, or, her for that matter.

With a sigh, Larry told the driver he was the only man to see Barstow die. "We were on the same B-17 that went down over Germany." Struck by the news, the driver pulled his pickup alongside the road and came to a stop. For an hour, the three men sat discussing Clarence, his last days in England, and that fateful day over Germany. When everything had been said that could be, the driver started up the truck again and they drove on in silence. Each man was wrapped in his private thoughts.

When the truck pulled off the highway at the turn into the village of Corry, the driver thanked Larry and wished him good luck. As he watched the truck drive away, Larry thought about the old and young Mrs. Barstows and their loss. He swallowed hard, turned, and stuck out his thumb.

Within a short time, Larry and Woody were picked up. Larry could see that Woody wanted to ask him something. Woody had stared at him a time or two in their travels, as if ready to ask something. But friends that they were, he respected Larry's privacy and never said a word. They never again talked about the ride to Corry or the war experience that Larry recounted inside that pickup on that summer day.

There were times when Larry wondered if he should have gone into Corry and met Clarence's mother and wife, but decided that it was probably for the best that a family friend broke the news to them. In his heart, Larry knew he was afraid to visit them.

Right after the war, an old army buddy told him about going to the Bronx in New York City to see his dead army buddy's family. When the airman introduced himself, the grieving mother started shrieking, crying, and asking why *he* was alive and not her son. The young airman dashed away as fast as he could. Larry knew he could not handle being put in a similar situation, so he never visited Clarence's mother or widow.

Years later, Larry's father forwarded a letter from Clarence's mother addressed to Larry. Mrs. Barstow said that she had received a letter from someone in Germany telling her that for seven hundred dollars Clarence's remains would be sent home for burial. Larry wrote back telling her to save her money and cautioned her that only the United States government brought back remains and provided coffins, not a civilian organization. He explained that the B-17 bomber burned upon impact and the intense heat would have destroyed Clarence's body. There would not have been any remains.

Larry told Mrs. Barstow that a German officer had shown him Clarence's blackened dog tags. The tags were so badly charred that he knew there couldn't possibly be any remains. Since Larry never heard from her again, he wasn't sure if she took his advice or not. It sickened him that people could be so cruel and pull such a scam on grieving families.

After Woody and Larry arrived in Erie, they found a 1941 Studebaker that Larry could just barely afford. In the new used car, he and Woody headed back to Clearfield. After a month of looking for work and finding nothing, Larry drove to Cleveland to see his old boss at the Goodyear Tire store about a job, and was promptly given one. However, after four months in the city, Larry decided to head back to the country and Pennsylvania. He found living among so many people unbearable. When Larry called home to talk to his father about his decision, Ivan told him that the coal mines were hiring drivers and, with a truck of his own, Larry could work for himself.

Back in Pennsylvania, Larry traded his car for a dump truck and hauled coal until threats from striking mineworkers made driving unsafe. During the war, the Roosevelt administration had

frozen wages and salaries. President Truman and the Wage Sta-
bilization Board still controlled wages in an effort to tame inflation in postwar America. After being patient for so many years,
labor unionists felt they were owed a wage increase. The United
Auto Workers went out on strike at plants near Detroit in
November of 1945. By 1946, electrical, radio, steel, and machine
workers had followed suit. Then in April, the United Mine
Workers demanded wage increases and a health and welfare
plan. When their demands were not met, they walked off the job.

For independent contractors, it was a difficult choice to make.
Many continued hauling coal. Striking workers, perched on
road overpasses, shot at the haulers. Larry began carrying a rifle
in his truck and rode in police escorts to and from the mine or
pit sites. He felt he was fighting another war, one with his own
people. The community was torn apart. Harassment came from
all sectors.

In the midst of all the difficulties, Larry met and married
Leona Maxine Le Grand in June 1946. The following year they
had a son, Lawrence Lee. With a family to support, he could not
afford to quit hauling. Frustrated and alarmed at the danger he
faced each day, Larry sold his truck. He needed to find a different job until the insanity calmed down and decided if he was
going to carry a gun he might as well join the army. Uncle Sam's
beckoning finger was not boring into his conscience. This time
the decision was totally his own.

In May of 1947, Larry Pifer reenlisted in the Army Air Corps.

Epilogue

After General Dwight Eisenhower demobilized his enormous military force created during WWII, the American services entered a new age in military preparedness. Air combat and the atomic age had arrived. Thousands of pilots with their planes returned from around the world to U.S. Army air bases.

On April 15, 1947, Larry Pifer drove to Geisetown, Pennsylvania, enlisted in the Army Reserves, and reported to Fort Slocum, New York for processing. In May, Pifer was discharged from the Reserves so that he could enlist in the Regular Army as a radio operator. He was assigned to a B-29 with the 306th Bomb Group at McDill Air Force Base in Tampa, Florida. However, a hurricane preempted this assignment and forced an evacuation of all bombers from Florida to Puerto Rico. While he was in Puerto Rico, orders came down for three of the radio operators to be sent to Castle Air Force Base in Atwater, California. The next day Pifer arrived in California not as a radio operator but as a gunner on a B-29 with Second Lieutenant Yentz and his crew, who were with the 330th Squadron in the 93rd Bomb Group. When his hitch was up in May of 1950, Pifer returned to Pennsylvania.

Pifer left active duty to become the owner of a gas station in York, Pennsylvania. However, as an army reservist and with the advent of the Korean War, he was called into active duty on January 11, 1951, and assigned to a fighter squadron. Pifer was discharged on October 10, 1952, as the war in Korea wound down. Within days of his discharge, Pifer chose to make the Army Air Force his career and flew to California to reenlist with a bomber outfit.

During his long and decorated career in the armed services, Pifer served in the U.S. Army Air Corps. When in 1956 it was divided into two branches, he became a member of the U.S. Air Force. During his service career, Pifer traveled from one American coast to the other and to air bases in Africa, Labrador, and Guam. Throughout his career, Pifer remained in the communications corps as a radio operator and instructor, but as a crew member flew on B-17s, B-29s, B-50s, and KC-97s. After serving during World War II, the Korean War, and the Cold War, Lawrence Pifer retired in August 1964 with two goals in mind: to own a farm and become a rural mail carrier.

In the 1930s, he had worked on neighboring farms during his summer break for extra income. As he toiled in the field one particularly sweltering summer day, he saw a rural mail carrier pass by. The idea of driving through the countryside instead of standing in a field, tired and sweaty, appealed to the teenager. Better yet, he decided that owning a farm and being a rural carrier would be the greatest things in life. However, it has been shown how fate interrupted his plans.

After retiring from the military, Larry returned to Pennsylvania to fulfill his dreams. Within a few months, he got a job with the U.S. Post Office in Woodland, Pennsylvania, as a rural carrier and was eventually assigned a permanent route in 1966. Each day, Larry drove his sixty-mile route through the countryside to places like Woodland, Bigler, Shiloh, Pleasant Valley, and

335th Bombardment Squadron, 95th Bomb Group (H), Eighth Air Force Veterans reunion in Cincinnati, Ohio, in 1986. The crew members of *Slightly Dangerous II* are in the first row. Left to right, Melvin B. Dunham, pilot; Lawrence Pifer, radio operator and ball-turret gunner; Marvin D. Anderson, flight engineer; and Warran A. Thompson, assistant radio operator. Courtesy of Lawrence Pifer.

New Egypt, delivering mail to 316 rural mail boxes. While on his route one day in 1973, he saw a sign advertising a farm for sale. Larry bought it. He and his wife, Maxine, moved from Woodland to the thirty-acre farm in Bradford Township to raise a few beef cattle and plant hay, oats, and corn. By the time Larry retired from the U.S. Post Office in 1978, he delivered to 495 boxes and made numerous friends along the way. For several years, Larry and Maxine worked the farm and enjoyed visits from their grandchildren. But after a heart attack in 1986, Larry was forced to cut back. In 1989, Larry and his wife sold their farm and bought a retirement home in Interlachen, Florida.

Larry Pifer still attends the World War II ex-prisoner-of-war encounter group at the Gainesville Veterans' Administration Hospital. Former POW Donald Kremper is also a member of the same group. While attending these meetings, Pifer and the group realized the significance of the story that they have to tell. Many have taken the opportunity to speak to groups at schools, club meetings, and reunions. Lawrence Pifer collaborated with his niece in writing this book. At this writing, there are only two survivors of the crew of *Slightly Dangerous II*, Robert Renner and Lawrence Pifer.

Appendix: Poems by Pows

During World War II, American prisoners of war in Germany wrote the poems that follow in this section. They are drawn from T/Sgt. Lawrence Pifer's logbook, mentioned earlier in the text. Pifer smuggled the logbook out of Stalag Luft 4 when the prisoners were evacuated on February 6, 1945. The logbook is worn, stained, and frayed, but the words found in it bespeak the adoration, the horrors, and the honor of the young men who were prisoners of war in Room 5 of Barracks 4 in Lager C in Stalag Luft 4.

There were many hours to fill in prison camp, during the day and the night. As a diversion, the men began to recite and write poetry in their logbooks. At first they would recite them aloud; then some of the men began to record them on paper. The poems recount their experiences in England, reveal their love and respect for their army buddies and their planes, and describe how it felt to be imprisoned in Germany. Fond of poetry, Pifer was intrigued by the prisoners' exercise and began to pencil their poems in his logbook. Eventually, back in the U.S., Pifer wrote a poem about his experience returning to civilian life, which also provided an ending to the logbook. Yes, he did have a hand in creating several of the poems, but claims authorship for only the last one. The poems are recorded exactly as they were found in the logbook.

A GUNNER'S DAY

A gunner's day is never done
Up at Dawn before the sun
With the roar of engines in his head
Wishing he could have stayed in bed

Chow at four, fried eggs and such
Won't have time to eat too much
Briefing at five, the crew is there
Anxious to be up in the air

See to your chutes, ammunition and guns
For the boys all know it's not for fun
Jerry will be there up in the blue
Waiting for someone, perhaps for you

Take-off at six or maybe six thirty
Hope no one has guns that are dirty
Form with the group at 12,00[0] feet
See that formation! It really looks neat

Put on your mask, the air's getting thin
Off to the battle, always with a grin
We're over the water, now test your guns
Enemy coast! Here comes the fun

Flak at six! Flak at twelve!
Lookout boys! They're giving us hell
Here come the fighters coming in low
Maybe they're ours, don't shoot till you know.

P-51S AND P-38S

Our escort is here. They're never late.
They're fighting fools each man and his ship.
There isn't a Jerry that they couldn't whip.

The air is cold just fifty below.
Turn up the heat, so you don't freeze a toe.
A sharp lookout, the target is near.
We don't want to meet the enemy here.

Target below plenty of flak.
Bombs away! Now we turn back.
Coming out of the sun enemy ships
Aim true. We've still got more trips.

There goes one down. Another one, too.
Our fighters are busy to see none get through.
There are flames in the sky, as another goes down.
The pilot bails out makes it safe to the ground.

Then in our tail the guns start to roar.
There's blood on your guns. You shoot as before.
Your ship is hit, but stays in the air.
You think of your loved ones or whisper a prayer.

Smoke from the target leaps high into the sky.
We'll show these Jerries we know how to fly.
The fighters have left us. The ones that were left.
Our fighters got some, we got the rest.

We've been up six hours; two hours to go.
Though we're doing 200 it seems very slow.
England at last we are all informed.
We think of our buddies who will never return.

We're over the field. The crew gives a sigh.
We've finished another, To Do or To Die.
Wheels touch the ground with a screech and a bump.
Our ship brought us back over the hump.

We're tired and dirty, thirst and sore.
The sun's gone down an hour before.
First clean your guns and do it good as before
That gun is life: his, mine or yours.

A sandwich and coffee. Your chute to turn in.
Down to the briefing room. Turn in your gun.
Two meals a day and both at night
Gets on your nerves but we're ready to fight.

The mess hall is warm in the cold of night.
You sit down to eat and talk between bites.
You talk of fighters, ours and theirs, too.
And of the boys who didn't get through.

Of ships going down, exploding in air,
The bullets that missed your head by a hair
Your ship's full of holes, Poor Joe is dead.
He caught a flak fragment in the side of the head!

Then head for your sack, about nine or ten.
A letter from home. Another from Ben.
I love you, she wrote. Then you know that you've won
For a gunner's day is never done.

MY BUDDY

They say he died in Glory
Whatever that may be

If dying in a burst of flame is glory
Then it's not for me.

In the briefing room that morning
He sat with clear eyes and strong heart
Just one of the many gunners
Determined to do his part.

My buddy had the guts all right
He sought neither glory nor fame
He knew he had a job to do
And his crew all felt the same.

But death had the final word
For in its log I wrote his name.
And my buddy died that morning
"In Glory" and a burst of flame.

WHAT WAS HIS NAME?

What was his name this lad so young
Who in silk and string his life was hung?
Oh yes, it did if I recall
The day he made that eternal fall.

What was his name this lad so brave
Who fought for his ship their life to save
There were many fighters with one desire
To see that "17" go down a-fire.

So in they came and did their best
There was the flame, it did the rest.
Over the phone came the pilot's shout,
Ok, Boys! Here's where we get out.

KRIEGIE FANTASY

You're up at eight in the morning
When you hear the breakfast call
It's German bread and brew you get
Believe me folks, that's all

Then a whistle sounds throughout the camp
And it's out to the counting grounds
Where the Jerries count you up and down
Like a pack of blood-thirsty hounds

The count is finished, we're all here
We then receive our dismiss
And it's back to the sack we go
To dream of the home we miss.

You're awakened by a whistle
"Brew's up" is the call
You hear the patter of running feet
Going down the barracks hall

You're not very excited
And neither are the rest
For it's Jerry coffee or hot water
And I swear it's not the best

When you walk out of the barracks
To absorb some air and sun
And look up in the sky so blue
And ask, "Is my job being done?"

You talk to pals and buddies
Of all the days gone by

And think of all your comrades
Still sitting in the sky

When you think of flying combat
Of hated fighters and bursting flak
Then you know that you'd trade anything
For a chance to just get back.

"Chows up" is the next call heard
You see a cook you knew
And ask what's on the menu
Is it barley or Jerry stew?

When your midday meal is over
And your cigarette is done
You take up playing ball or cards
Just to have some fun.

You have another brew at three
And your heart begins to swell
I've helped to keep the folks at home
Away from this living hell.

They count you again at five o'clock
Double checking on us you see
Making sure that some of us
Haven't gambled to be free.

When the evening count is over
And the supper whistle blows
You give a yell at the detail men
To make sure they're on their toes.

Then another meal of barley or stew
And you run and rave and cuss
Until another rumour comes in
That our troops will soon rescue us.

Then the blackout boards are set in place
And the fat you start to chew
Of days gone by when you and yours
Were fighting in the blue.

Into the hands of *Morpheus* you fall
Saying they can't do this to me
But gloating softly to yourself
"Thank God our Nations Free."

THE BALTIC CRUISE

That sea of stricken faces
That we saw down below
We can't express our feelings
But we won't forget I know

We climbed down the ladder
Below the water line
While Jerry was riding up on top
Where everything was fine

A prayer was on our lips we know
No Hypocrites were there
The sweat rolled off our bodies
All were stripped down bare.

Your husband, son, or sweetheart
Was maybe in there too

But did he complain? "No, Sir"
His thought[s] were still on you

If I can spare you torture
I won't say a word
Everyone must have thought the same
For not a sound was heard.

A little drink of water
Doesn't seem much to you
And a ray of fresh sunshine
Or a sky of velvet blue

But take them all away folks
And their value is very high
That's what happened on that boat
And we were all prepared to die.

Forty-eight hours of hell on earth
We rode the stormy sea
Ten men were crowded in a space
Where one man ought to be.

We suffered torture and hunger
But we didn't hear a sigh
The stronger prayed for courage
The weaker prayed to die.

Although we're not complaining
We'll take it like a man
But we'll always remember
When we're back home again.

One prisoner weaker than the rest
Who just could stand no more
Jumped overboard that stormy nite
And tried to swim ashore.

But wait a minute, "What was that?"
The silence broken by a shot
A watery grave in the Baltic Sea
Was that poor prisoner's lot.

So when you start complaining
And your pleasures seem so few
Just think of the boys from Stalag 6
And what we all went through.

So buck up, That's the spirit
And when the war is done
We'll all come marching home again
Without our pack and gun.

PILGRIMS OF ETERNITY

By Lawrence I. Pifer

They had come home from the wars
and the wars had returned with them.
Parents rejoiced, bands blared,
And everyone joined in laughter.

Children made them heroes,
Adults acclaimed them saviors
Nations sighed, relieved.
They were their family's pride
And were escorted from house to house and
consequently displayed.

Accepting the toast, denying flattery
Playing the role of the polite
With a smile, a curt "Thank you."
They endured the "prying host."
But soon the mothers awarded
The changes in their sons were obvious.
Youth, Ah! Where was their youth?
Their laughter? And, too, their humor.
Why, now thought the mothers,
Are they somber? Are they pensive?
To watch them absently gazing into space
Or apparently studying the hearth
With tired eye and knitted brow
Speaking only when spoken to
And even then not always.

Mothers remember and grow old.
The home that waited for their return
And the return of ringing laughter
And mischievous pranks
And the good nite kiss.

The ball and bat are recalled
Now sealed with spider's web.
Yes, destroy that web if you will
But that spirit will defy repossession.
Defy it, now and forever.

And the question, what is in their minds?
Means but "why now be they cynics?"
Why is it said, "All is well?"
Why do they smile so sad, so grim?
That we know all is not well.

And that reason "why"
Lies hidden in their learning of truth.

Oh, People!
There were haunting memories
Memories tragic of another world
Of another time.
They perhaps recalled what you forgot
Or things to you unknown.
Perhaps their hearts and souls
And vast accumulation of knowledge
Lay in their visions of death.

In some blinking memory of the past
A corpse, rigid in the pool
Of adulterated rain, mud and blood
With its mouth open to speak
And with eyes fixed heavenward
Was the summation of their silence.

And so night would fall
And with some mumbled excuse
They would depart from home
And begin their search
Up and down the streets of childhood.

All familiar, agonizingly so
For still all was strange
They knew of a change.
Because these streets, on which long ago,
They had run and laughed
As innocents in short pants
Would not echo, even that laughter again.

They roam to the ballpark
To seek recollections there
But only defeat meets them.
There were no phantom friends
To imagine among the shadows.
No crack of bat, nor thud of ball.
No youthful sound to the tensioned ear.

Then they ambled on in dejection
To meet a childhood acquaintance.
To feel the surge of hope
But to realize futility.
And so [they] perform a simple ceremony,
The offertory of cigarettes,
The flash of a match in the darkness,
The consecration of a sacred memory,
And the parting, both in communion,
Of a mutual knowledge.

Home again to mount the stairs
With a deliberate goodnite and then
To dream those damnable dreams!

Sweethearts too awarded.
They couldn't trace the old love.
The life was gone from the old love.

They [too had] found a 'new love.'
A woman more enchanting;
A woman who they feared
Whom they counted for months
They found suffering in his absence
They realized that this worthless woman

Could administer mercy and compassion
And perhaps they could receive [from] [her] things
If they learned to love her.

Her 'whoredom' was 'gratis' and inevitable
For men had seen a stricken friend
Plead for her merciful touch
As he lay upon a crimson deck, or another
Receive her kiss, as he plummeted
From the heavens in flames.

No, sweetheart, their love for you did not die
But she had proven her works
And they knew that in the end
They were destined to be hers.

So tragic and unexplainable it was
They had come home from the wars
And the wars had returned with them.
They knew all and spoke nothing
For they knew among other things the futility of words
And the mass chaos of life.

They accepted untruth with resignation and yet,
After the fall of each twilight
They would go out and walk again.

NOTES

FOREWORD

1. Norman Mailer, *The Naked and the Dead* (New York, Rinehart, 1948); James Jones, *From Here to Eternity* (New York: Scribner, 1951); Robert Lee Scott, *God Is My Co-Pilot* (Garden City, N.Y.: Blue Ribbon Books, 1944); Kurt Vonnegut, *Slaughterhouse Five* (New York: Dell Publishing Co., 1969); James Michener, *Tales of the South Pacific* (New York: Macmillan, 1947).

2. Edward Beattie, Jr., *Diary of a Kriegie* (New York: Thomas Y. Crowell Co., 1946); Alan Newcomb, *Vacation with Pay: Being an Account of My Stay at the German Rest Camp for Tired Allied Airmen at Beautiful Barth-on-the-Baltic* (Haverhill, Mass.: Destiny Publishing, 1947); Francis Sampson, *Paratrooper Padre* (Sweetwater, Tenn.: 101 Airborne Division Association, 1948); John Vietor, *Time Out: American Airmen at Stalag Luft I* (New York: R. R. Smith, 1951; Falbrook, Calif.: Aero Publishers, 1984).

3. See, for example, "Stalag Luft I," "Stalag II-B," and "Stalag IV-B," in "Folders, Camp Reports–Germany," RG 389, National Archives, Modern Military Branch, Washington, D.C.; "Oflag 64," "Stalag Luft VI," and "Reports of POW Camps, 1944-1945," RG 332, Washington National Record Center, Suitland, Md.; David C. Howard, *A Kriegie Log* (502.13-1), and Col. Charles G. Goodrich, "History of the USAAF Prisoners of War of the South Compound, Stalag Luft III, September 1943–April

1945" (506.616A), at the Air Force Historical Research Center, Maxwell AFB, Montgomery, Alabama.

4. Edward Dobran, *P.O.W.: The Story of an American Prisoner of War during World War Two* (New York: Exposition Press, 1953); Eric Williams, *The Book of Famous Escapes: A Chronicle of Escape in Many Wars with Eighteen First-Hand Accounts* (New York: W. W. Norton, 1954).

5. Florimond Duke, with Charles Swaart, *Name, Rank, and Serial Number* (New York: Meredith Publishers, 1969); A. J. Barker, *Prisoners of War* (New York: Universe Books, 1975); James F. Stone, *A Holiday in Hitlerland* (New York: Carlton Press, 1970).

6. John G. Hubbell, *P.O.W.: A Definitive History of the American Prisoner-of-War Experience in Vietnam, 1964–1973* (New York: Readers Digest Press, 1976).

7. David A. Foy, *For You the War Is Over: American Prisoners of War in Nazi Germany* (New York: Stein & Day, 1984); E. B. Kerr, *Surrender and Survival: The Experience of American POWs in the Pacific, 1941–1945* (New York: W. Morrow, 1985); David Westheimer, *Sitting It Out: A World War II POW Memoir* (Houston: Rice University Press, 1992); Robert C. Doyle, *Voices from Captivity: Interpreting the American POW Narrative* (Lawrence, Kans.: University Press of Kansas, 1994).

CHAPTER 1: THE EARLY YEARS

1. Arthur M. Schlesinger, Jr., ed., *The Almanac of American History* (New York: Brompton Books Corp., 1993), 475.

CHAPTER 2: BASIC TRAINING

1. Schlesinger, *Almanac of American History*, 446, and Norman Polmar and Thomas B. Allen, *World War II: America at War, 1941–1945* (New York: Random House, 1991), 839. Background material in this chapter is taken from the Schlesinger and Polmar and Allen books.

CHAPTER 4: INTO BATTLE

1. In 1994, Florence Bittner completed a manuscript entitled "War Experiences" that outlined the military exploits of her husband's tour in World War II. Drawing from Fred's letters to her and his parents, letters from other crew members, and histories of the 95th Bombardment

Group and the Eighth Air Force, Bittner recounted Fred's experiences with the crew of *Slightly Dangerous*.

CHAPTER 5: *SLIGHTLY DANGEROUS II*

1. Bittner, 60.
2. Ibid., 62.
3. Barry Smith letter to author, August 19, 1997.

CHAPTER 6: THE LAST MISSION

1. Ronald H. Bailey, *The Air War in Europe* (Alexandria, Va.: Time-Life Book, 1981), 158.
2. Barry Smith letter to Melvin Dunham, August 21, 1997.

CHAPTER 8: CAPTURED

1. Figures and quotes were gathered from newspaper clippings found in Helen (Pifer) Snyder's scrapbook, kept during World War II and later presented to her brother, Lawrence Pifer. Articles are dated, but newspapers are not identified. However, a majority of the articles are from the *Kingston (New York) Daily Freeman*.

CHAPTER 9: DULAG LUFT FRANKFURT

1. Numbers were compiled from reports prepared by the Military Intelligence Service of the War Department for the period July 1944 through November 1945.

CHAPTER 11: A KRIEGIE'S DAY

1. Sgt. Robert Doherty's report of the boxing matches in Stalag Luft 6, World War II Stalag Luft and POW Camps can be found at http://www.b24.net/pow/stalag6.htm.

CHAPTER 14: STALAG LUFT 4

1. Donald Kremper letter to author, November 26, 2000, and section from his 2000 manuscript regarding the Military Government Tribunals and the United Nations War Crimes Commission, undated.

CHAPTER 15: LIFE IN CAMP

1. Charcoal such as Pifer described is a hard wood that has smoldered until forming a hard briquette.

CHAPTER 19: GOING HOME

1. "Rationing in World War II," U.S. Office of Price Administration (Washington, D.C., November 1946), 1.

BIBLIOGRAPHY

AUTHOR'S INTERVIEWS AND CORRESPONDENCE

Kremper, Donald. Letters to author. 26 November 2000, 3 March 2002, and 4 May 2002.

Pifer, Lawrence. Interview by the author. Tape recording. Interlachen, Fla., 13–16 January 1998.

———. Telephone interview by the author. 22 January 1998.

———. Telephone interview by the author. 27 December 1998.

———. Interview by the author. 29–31 July 2001.

———. Telephone interview by the author. 19, 23 August 2001.

———. Telephone interview by the author. 17 September 2001.

———. Telephone interview by the author. 2 October 2001.

———. Interview by the author. 1–3 May 2002.

Smith, Barry. Letters to author. 19 August 1997 and 1 July 2002.

DOCUMENTS

American National Red Cross. Map of location of German camps and hospitals. 31 December 1944.

———. Map of prisoner-of-war and civilian internee camps in Europe. June 1945.

National Archives and Records Administration. Center for Electronic Records. World War II POW Report. Lawrence I. Pifer file. Printed August 1, 2000.

Pifer, Lawrence. Logbook. Winter 1945.

———. Embarkation Papers. 1945.

———. AAF Technical School Yearbook, Sioux Falls, S. Dak. November 1942.

———. Harlingen (Texas) Army Gunnery School Certificate of Proficiency. 2 January 1943.

———. Army Air Force Certificate for Radio Operators and Mechanics. 21 November 1942.

———. Military Pass for Gowen Field, Boise, Id. 22 January 1943.

———. Military Pass for Walla Walla, Wash. 29 March 1943.

———. Letter from Helen Pifer Snyder to Lawrence Pifer, 1944.

———. Lawrence Pifer to Dan Acieta. 25 December 1943.

———. Letters from Lawrence Pifer to Helen Pifer Snyder. 12 December 1944, January 1945.

———. Prisoner-of-War post from Helen Pifer Snyder to Lawrence Pifer, 1944.

———. Ex-POW field postcard from T/Sgt. Lawrence Pifer to Helen Pifer Snyder. 7 May 1945.

———. Western Union telegram from T/Sgt. Lawrence Pifer to Helen Pifer Snyder. 16 May 1945.

———. Western Union telegram from T/Sgt. Lawrence Pifer to Helen Pifer. 16 May 1945.

———. Lawrence Rose to Lawrence Pifer. Date unknown.

Snyder, Helen Pifer. Scrapbook, 1940–45.

U.S. Office of Price Administration. Rationing in World War II. November 1946.

U.S. War Department. Military Intelligence Service. American Prisoners of War in Germany. Dulag Luft and Stalag Luft 4 and 6. 15 July 1944.

———. Military Intelligence Service. American Prisoners of War in Germany. Transit Camp, Section of Dulag Luft. 1 November 1945.

———. Office of the Commanding General Army Service Forces. German Orders. 1941.

———. Headquarters Army Service Forces, Office of the Provost Marshal General. "Revised Mailing Instructions—Germany." March 1944 and Revised Form, 1 June 1944.

NEWSPAPERS

Barbed Wire News (Stalag Luft 6). May 1944.

Heritage Herald: The Official Newsletter of the Aerospace Heritage Foundation of Utah. Vol. 3, no. 3. Third Quarter 2001.

Kingston (New York) Daily Freeman. 8 March 1944.

Sykesville, (Pa.) Post-Dispatch. 7 April 1944.

Rochester (New York) Tribune. Date Unknown.

MANUSCRIPTS

American Prisoners of War in Germany. Testimony of Dr. Leslie Kaplan. Prepared by the War Crimes Office, Civil Affairs Division, WDSS. 31 December 1947.

Anonymous. "From Silk to Wire." TS (photocopy).

Bittner, Florence. "War Experiences of Fred Bittner." TS (photocopy). 1994 (?).

Dirickson, Louis W. Untitled manuscript. TS (photocopy). Date unknown.

Dunham, Melvin. "The First American Berlin Raid." TS (photocopy). Date unknown.

Kremper, Donald. Portions of untitled manuscript and drawings. TS (photocopy). Date unknown.

O'Donnell, Joseph P. "The Shoe Leather Express, Book II Luftgangsters." TS (photocopy). October 1986.

BOOKS AND MAGAZINES

Bailey, Ronald H. *Prisoners of War*. Alexandria, Va.: Time-Life Books, 1981.

———. *The Air War in Europe*. Alexandira, Va.: Time-Life Books, 1981.

Baybutt, Ron. *Colditz: The Great Escapes*. Boston: Little, Brown, 1982.

Beltrone, Art and Lee. *A Wartime Log*. Charlottesville, Va.: Howell Press, 1994.

Biggs, Chester M. *Behind Barbed Wire: Memoir of a World War II U.S. Marine*. Jefferson, N.C.: McFarland & Co. Inc., 1995.

Carlson, Lewis H. *We Were Each Other's Prisoners: An Oral History of World War II American and German Prisoners of War*. New York: Basic-Books, 1997.

Charles, H. Robert. *Last Men Out*. Austin, Tex.: Eakin Press, 1988.

"Geographic's New Map of Germany and Its Approaches," *National Geographic* 86, no. 1 (July 1944): 66–72.

Grady, Frank, and Rebecca Dickson. *Surviving the Day: An American Prisoner of War in Japan*. Annapolis, Md.: Naval Institute Press, 1997.

Guderley, George. "Lest We Forget," *Air Force Magazine* 80, no. 9 (September 1997).

Hammond's Library Atlas of the World. New York: C. S. Hammond, 1943.

Hawkins, Ian. *Courage, Honor and Victory*. Winston-Salem, N.C.: Hunter Publishing Co., 1987.

―――. *B-17s over Berlin: Personal Stories from the 95th Bomb Group* (H). Washington, D.C.: Brassey's, 1990.

Lewis, Bruce. *Four Men Went to War*. New York: St. Martin's Press, 1987.

Messenger, Charles. *The Chronological Atlas of World War Two*. New York: Macmillan, 1989.

Microsoft Encarta Encyclopedia 2001. General Eisenhower. 1993–2000 Microsoft Corporation.

Monahan, Evelyn M., and Rosemary Neidel-Greenlee. *All This Hell: U.S. Nurses Imprisoned by the Japanese*. Lexington: University Press of Kentucky, 2000.

O'Neill, Brian D. *Half a Wing, Three Engines and a Prayer: B–17s over Germany*. New York: McGraw-Hill, 1998, 1999.

Polmar, Norman, and Thomas B. Allen. *World War II: America at War, 1941–1945*. New York: Random House, 1991.

Schneider, Sam, ed. *This Is How It Was: 485th Bomb Group (Heavy) Unit History*. St. Petersburg, Fla.: Southern Heritage Press, 1995.

Schlesinger, Arthur M., ed. *The Almanac of American History*. New York: Brompton Books Corp., 1993.

Smith, Stanley W. *Prisoner of the Emperor: An American POW in World War II*. Edited by Duane A. Smith. Niwot, Colo.: University of Colorado Press, 1991.

INTERNET

"History of B-17." 3 March 2000: n.p. On-line. Available *http://www. letadla. pinknet.cz/b17/hist.html.*

"B-17." 3 October 1998. On-line. Available *http://www.af.mil/photos/Oct 1997/ b17blue.html.*

"Boeing B-17 in Flight." 14 August 1998. On-line. Available *http://www. carlisle-www.army.mil/cgi-bin/usam.*

"Cigarette Camps: The U.S. Army Camps in the LeHavre Area." 28 July 2001. On-line. Available *http://www.skylighters.org/special/cigcamps/ cigmaps.html.*

Hatton, Greg. "Dulag Luft." B24.NET. 27 September 2000. On-line. Available *http://www.b24.net/pow/dulag.html.*

The International Committee of the Red Cross and the Second World War. "Geneva Convention of 27 July 1929 Relative to the Treatment of Prisoners of War." 29 March 2001. On-line. Available *http://www. icrc.org/icrceng.nsf.*

———. "The Central Agency for Prisoners of War." 29 March 2001. On-line. Available *http://www.icrc.org/icrceng.nsf.*

———. "General Introduction." 29 March 2001. On-line. Available *http:// www. icrc.org/icrceng.nsf.*

"381st Bomb Group (Heavy)." 1 August 2001. On-line. Available *http:// www. 381st.org/images_maps–england.html.*

http://www.381st.org/images_missionbrief.html.

http://www.381st.org/images_hangers.html.

http://www.381st.org/images_messhall.html.

http://www.381st.org/images_interrogation.html.

ACKNOWLEDGMENTS

I am grateful to many people who contributed to my research and helped me to complete this book. I particularly want to thank my uncle, Lawrence Pifer. I am very grateful for the more than forty hours of interview time that he allowed me. During many phone calls across the country to his homes in Florida and Pennsylvania we discussed fine points and revisions. I appreciate the hours that he and my aunt, Maxine, took to search for and provide valuable primary source material, photographs, and ephemera from those years before, during, and after the war. Thank you, Uncle Larry, for all those late night hours; for taking me to the National Prisoner of War Museum in Andersonville, Georgia, twice; for taking me to air shows so that I might climb in and go through a World War II "Flying Fortress"; for patiently sitting through photography sessions; and for the stories. Without you, this book would never have come to fruition.

I sincerely want to thank Helen Pifer Snyder for keeping a scrapbook during the war years and presenting it so generously to her brother so many years later. I want to thank Donald Kremper for freely sharing his research notes, photographs, and sketches of Stalag Luft 6 and 4, which helped to document more fully the lives of the American prisoners of war in Germany. In addition, Barry Smith supplied me with information on the German Sturmstaffel 1 and photographs of the actual pilots whose actions brought down *Slightly Dangerous II*. I am grateful to Bob Plisk for patiently explaining cartography and designing the map. Thank you, Roger Whitacre, for the excellent photographs of the escape map.

Next I wish to thank friends and colleagues who helped in many and various ways. I thank the Friday Afternoon Writing Group and Christine Whitacre for encouraging me to present this manuscript to a larger audience than just the family. Thank you to Donna Kadish and her sixth-grade pupils who thought this book was exciting to listen to, even in a rough state. I wish to thank T. F. Poduska, who read early portions of the book and offered insights. Others who contributed include Bob Poduska, Florence Van Bebber, Charles and Irene Kuhl, Susan and Tom Carlson, Richard Stensgaard, Jerry Greene, and especially Heather Thomas, who encouraged me to write.

I would like to thank my editor, Charles E. Rankin, for taking a chance on an idea and helping me shape and focus the manuscript into its final form. Thank you, Chuck.

I also appreciated the support of my family, Jon, Jared, and Juli, who saw more of the back of my head at my desk than the rest of me during the various stages of this book. Thanks, too, to my mother, Patricia Trimble, for her love and support during the difficult times. I especially want to thank my husband, John Bunyak, for giving me the courage to realize a dream.

INDEX